Take
This Book
to Work

Also by Tory Johnson and Robyn Freedman Spizman
Women For Hire's Get-Ahead Guide to Career Success

Also by Robyn Freedman Spizman
The GIFTionary: An A–Z Reference Guide for Solving
Your Gift-Giving Dilemmas . . . Forever!

Make It Memorable: An A–Z Guide to Making
Any Event, Gift, or Occasion . . . Dazzling!

Take This Book to Work

How to Ask for (and Get) Money, Fulfillment, and Advancement

Tory Johnson and
Robyn Freedman Spizman

St. Martin's Griffin

NEW YORK

TAKE THIS BOOK TO WORK. Copyright © 2006 by Women For Hire, LLC, and Robyn Freedman Spizman Literary Works, LLC. All rights reserved. Printed in the United States of America. No part of this book may be used or reproduced in any manner whatsoever without written permission except in the case of brief quotations embodied in critical articles or reviews. For information, address St. Martin's Press, 175 Fifth Avenue, New York, N.Y. 10010.

www.stmartins.com

Book design by Gretchen Achilles

Library of Congress Cataloging-in-Publication Data

Johnson, Tory.
    Take this book to work : how to ask for (and get) money, fulfillment, and advancement / Tory Johnson and Robyn Freedman Spizman.
        p. cm.
    ISBN-13: 978-0-312-35886-0
    ISBN-10: 0-312-35886-5
    1. Career development. 2. Vocational guidance for women. I. Spizman, Robyn Freedman. II. Title. III. Title: How to ask for (and get) money, fulfillment, and advancement.

HF5382.6.J63 2006
650.1—dc22

2006046456

First St. Martin's Griffin Edition: September 2007

10 9 8 7 6 5 4 3 2 1

To smart, talented women at every level and in all industries—
we encourage you to speak up for what you want at work.

Contents

Money

Getting Hired

On the Job

Professional Advancement

Onward and Upward

Personal Fulfillment

Time Management, Flexibility, and Personal Issues

Acknowledgments

We wish to extend our sincerest thanks to the women who shared their knowledge and insights and whose advice appears throughout this book. To our dedicated literary agent, Meredith Bernstein, who supported our vision of a book to encourage women to learn how to speak up at work and who spoke up on our behalf. To Jennifer Enderlin, our outstanding editor, who championed our book and secured a yes. We thank you for your bright ideas, smart insights, and clear vision for this book. Our thanks also go to the talented team at St. Martin's–Griffin, including Kimberly Cardascia, publicity guru John Karle, Jenny Carrow, David Stanford Burr, and Paul Montazzoli. Our appreciation to Jill Westfall and Marsha Pelzer for their helpful research. Our deepest thanks for the outstanding contributions and expertise of the following people and organizations: Catalyst, the leading research and advisory organization on women in business, on finding a mentor; Robert Damon, president, North America for Korn/Ferry International, on negotiating a severance package; Susan Filkins, Coordinator, Alumni Programs, Center for Career Services at Syracuse University, on maximizing alumni contacts; Dr. Kathleen Hall, author of *A Life in Balance: Nourishing the Four Roots of True Happiness*, on asking for flexibility; Marisa Thalberg, founder of Executive Moms, on staying connected during maternity leave; Carolyn N. Turknett, coauthor of *Decent People, Decent Company: How to Lead with Character at Work and in Life*, on seeking more responsibility; and David Williams, president and chief executive officer of Make-A-Wish Foundation of America, on getting companies to support charitable causes. Your time and knowledge will benefit so many women. Our thanks also goes to Jennifer Jones and John P. Schreitmueller for their valuable insights.

FROM TORY JOHNSON: My husband Peter, our children Emma, Jake, and Nick, and my brother, David cheer me on at every turn. They make my work worthwhile. I'm also very grateful to the many smart, strong, and supportive women in my life— Evelyn Goldstein, Sherry Beilinson, Donna Weitz, Stella Johnson, Margaret Johnson, Julie Zerring, Jodi Goldman, Dora Dvir, Lara Hall, Stephanie Biasi, Amanda Donikowski, Michelle Atkins, Jennifer Ryder, Lindsay Weitz, and Tess Johnson. I can't say thank-you enough to everyone at *Good Morning America* for their exceptional work ethic and for giving me the privilege of offering career advice to millions of viewers throughout the country.

FROM ROBYN SPIZMAN: There is a long list of amazing family members, friends, and colleagues who serve as gifts in my life, having answered my endless requests over the years. These are the precious folks who cheer me on to victory, and I am heavily indebted to them. Thank you for your love, friendship, help, knowledge, and more—this book is dedicated to you. To my devoted husband, Willy, and our wonderful children, Justin and Ali—I couldn't ask for a greater support team. Thank you for being the most loving family a girl could have. To my parents, Phyllis and Jack Freedman—you are my ongoing inspiration. You taught me that it's okay to ask. To my brother, Doug and his wife, Genie; to Sam and Gena, Aunt Lois Blonder, Aunt Ramona Freedman, and my beloved family members who are looking over us and are deeply missed, plus the rest of my family; and to my incredible friends—you all know who you are! And to the Spizman Agency, especially Jenny Corsey for your amazing help and fabulous assistance; and a thank-you around the clock to Bettye Storne, my guardian angel at work, who always knows what I want before I even ask!

Introduction

If I had only asked! Perhaps this phrase sounds familiar. You probably know firsthand how hard it is to ask for what you want at work. Ask and you shall receive? Surely we all know it's not that easy, especially in the cutthroat world of work.

We polled more than 500 professional women, some of them looking for a job and some happily employed, on what they viewed as the biggest hot-button issues with which they routinely struggle. Three topics consistently emerged: money, professional advancement, and personal fulfillment. Regardless of their industry, occupation, or level of success, most working women throughout the country had these issues at the top of their minds. As we dug deeper, we discovered a specific thread at the core of each of these workplace challenges: it all came down to what an individual did to prepare and then was willing or able to ask for.

Whether they're seeking employment for the first time or simply trying to advance their careers after years on the job, many women routinely grapple with how to ask for what they want and feel they have earned through hard work and commitment. But often we don't ask questions because we're shy, intimidated, or simply uncomfortable. Other times, we just don't feel like we're entitled to ask, or we allow a fear of looking stupid—and/or a feeling of self-consciousness to hold us back. It often boils down to an uncertainty about the timing, protocol, and even specific language to use when asking specifically for what we want. In the end, many women wind up sitting on the situation, stalling and stewing instead of asking.

Our research uncovered feelings of regret from the endless women who recalled not asking for that well-deserved promotion, overdue raise, additional training, much-needed time off, or available perk that they later learned other women and men received. In contrast, we also learned that tenacious women who did speak up for what they wanted at work were more successful and more content in their careers.

Of course, that's not to say that all your requests will be granted, appreciated, or even heard. While we encourage you to ask for what you want, we certainly know you won't always get it. However, initiating a dialogue and filling it with smart questions that are grounded in knowledge increase the possibility that you will succeed in reaching your goals.

Asking the essential questions is an important life skill, one that any woman can master quickly. *Take This Book to Work* will be your guide to learning it. This book paves your way to successful workplace communication by offering you specific tactics and strategies that will leave you feeling ready to ask for it and satisfied that you did. It's written in an easy-to-follow format with straight-forward advice, as opposed to hard-to-decipher theory. You will learn:

- The do's and don'ts of how to ask well-thought-out questions

- How to approach someone in person, by e-mail, and by phone

- What not to ask and why

- Ways to promote your case when asking for the things you believe you deserve

- How to anticipate opposition so that you are poised to respond when someone says no

As the CEO of Women For Hire, the leading producer of the only high-caliber career expos and recruitment services for professional women and top employers, and as a nationally known consumer advocate dedicated to helping make women smarter and better—with more than five decades of tackling the career world between us—we set forth to consider all the everyday and not-so-everyday situations that women face regardless of job description or title. We canvassed the country to determine the questions women wished they knew how to ask, and on the following pages we share the tactics and strategies that will help you conquer the words and actions necessary to catapult your career to success.

Keep in mind the importance of body language when asking for anything at work. Even the most thoroughly rehearsed arguments will fall on deaf ears if you're averting your eyes, chomping on chewing gum, or swaying back and forth. Stumbling over words or forgetting what you wanted to say does not communicate confidence and suggests you are not secure with your request. So, like with any important presentation or conversation that a great deal rests upon, practice what you want to say, boil it down to a succinct message and don't lose sight of why you are asking and the importance of your request. When asking for something, focus on the areas you can control: have all your ducks in a row, feel good about yourself, select the right time, stand or sit tall, deliver a firm handshake, and maintain direct eye contact.

Reversing Rejection

There will be times when you ask for something, and the answer you're given is no. Instead of walking away empty-handed, look for ways to turn that no into a maybe—and, ultimately, into a yes. Sometimes no is simply a request for more information. When someone says no to you, it's often an opportunity for you to ask why they're hesitant about approving your request. Attempt to uncover what is at the root of this rejection. This process can help you to determine an appropriate course of follow-up, which may include additional information and questions that will strengthen your case.

Take the example of a woman who applied for a human resources position at an accounting firm. She had performed a similar role in recruiting for a medical devices manufacturer and for a technology company. The hiring manager at the accounting firm thanked her for applying, but said they weren't interested in pursuing her candidacy. He wished her well.

Instead of accepting the rejection, the woman asked why they were hesitant to interview her, especially since she knew she was ideally suited for the position. The manager admitted that they really wanted someone with industry knowledge, not just recruiting experience. The applicant pointed out that she excelled in her two previous positions even though she started both with no knowledge of their businesses. What she possesses, she argued, was much more important: the ability to identify and recruit the best talent to the companies. She felt strongly that she could learn the basics of the business because she's a quick study.

The hiring manager agreed, and he arranged for her to interview with his firm. When the applicant aced the interviews, she received a job offer, thereby having turned the initial no into a maybe and then into a yes.

If you get weak at the knees just thinking about speaking up with confidence and poise, consider joining a Toastmaster's group or signing up for a public speaking course. Such programs can empower you with specific steps to improve your skills. You'll also have the chance to observe other capable women who can serve as role models for strong communications.

When you've done your research and you're well prepared, you need not worry about appearing foolish with your requests for advancement in the workplace. Your only fear should come from refusing to speak up for what you want and deserve. When you remain silent in the face of inequities, you give other people permission to take advantage of you. Asking for change—insisting on it, in fact—is the best solution.

Go ahead, ask for it!

Tory Johnson (womenforhire.com) and Robyn Freedman Spizman (robynspizman.com)

Money

Getting Hired

How to Ask If a Company Is Hiring

It's helpful to have information about a particular company's current hiring needs, whether it's from online postings, newspaper advertisements, or even an employee of the company who knows what her department is looking for. However, not every company has a career section on its Web site, advertises its openings, and keeps you updated on its needs. In fact, many small and medium-sized companies don't do any of this. So how do you ask if they're hiring or have openings?

WHOM SHOULD YOU PURSUE? If there's a company you've been eyeing, do some research on its struggles and its potential for growth. Online searches, media coverage, and industry-specific networking may reveal a lot about the needs and strengths of a particular company. That information could indicate opportunities for employment.

Additionally, in your daily newspaper, you may read about a company that is expanding in your city, and this information could spark your interest in exploring possible positions. You might walk the mall and discover a new store that's about to open and will need to make hires.

Let's say that you are thinking of looking for a new position and find yourself at a party or industry event. The conversation is so fascinating that you start dreaming about joining their organization. In such a case, you can say, "While I'm not yet actively searching for a new position, I'm so intrigued by what your company is doing. Might you suggest the right person for me to connect with to determine what possibilities exist for employment? I'd welcome the chance to see if there's mutual interest."

Announcements about new appointments to senior positions are a good way to spot potential openings. While you might not have seen any openings for a particular publication, you recently read that a new editor-in-chief was named at a great magazine. Send a note congratulating her and inquire about work. "I was delighted to read about your appointment since I've been a subscriber for several years. I know that every new manager likes to make her mark by bringing in fresh talent. I'm hoping you'll be willing to consider me for some writing assignments once you're ready to plan your first batch of articles."

The bottom line is to be alert and aware of the information and people you encounter. This can lead to a range of opportunities even if a specific position isn't obvious from the onset. When you spot something you'd like to pursue, don't make the mistake of sending a generic letter addressed to no one. You must determine to whom your inquiry should be specifically addressed. Call the receptionist or head of human resources at the company that has piqued your interest, and ask her who is handling hiring decisions. If you're told that there are no current needs, try reaching out to the person who heads up the division you want to work for. "I recently read about your expansion in Latin American markets. I have extensive international experience that could prove to be a great asset to your plans. I'm hoping you'll be willing to set up a time to meet when we can talk about potential openings or even consulting assignments. If you're not the right person to handle this, perhaps you'd be so kind as to tell me whom I can reach out to by phone or e-mail?"

OVERLOOKED OPPORTUNITIES. Part-time, freelance, and consulting jobs are some of the main types of positions that are usually not posted or advertised. If the company is one you really want to join, find out how to contact the person in charge, human resources, or the department you want to be a part of. When you make your contact, share the highlights of your abilities and experience and ask if there are freelance opportunities suitable to your skills. This option works best for more-senior positions that aren't necessarily advertised because there is no head count or budget for a full-time staffer. However, a department head is often able and willing to make provisions to bring on consultants. These positions can be lucrative in themselves and can turn into full-time roles. Again, since these options aren't advertised, you'll need to inquire about them by taking the initiative.

Have a pleasant, strong, and concise pitch ready to offer as to why you're calling. If you get an assistant, you can say, "I know from reading the article in *Crain's* that Mr. Lerner is leading the expansion to the West Coast. While his hiring plans might not yet be firm, I wanted the opportunity to connect with him about possible freelance work since I have extensive experience and success in this area. When would be a convenient time for me to speak with him? Or do you think it would be best for me to send him an e-mail detailing my experience and interests? I am confident he will thank you for this lead."

How to Ask If Your Résumé Has Been Received

Your résumé is the marketing tool that helps you get your foot in the door. You've worked tirelessly on making it perfect, so don't spoil your efforts and abandon your chances for landing an interview by not following up. Not only will a prompt follow-up increase your chances for an interview, it will also prove to your prospective employer that you are interested in a specific position. This step separates you from the people who simply submit dozens and dozens of résumés without having any particular passion for or interest in a role, in hope that one of them will elicit a response.

Every job seeker knows that you often submit résumés without hearing anything in return. You wind up sitting by the phone or computer desperate to know if the human resources people have received your résumé, especially since you can't just call up and say, "Hey, did you get it or not?"

Résumés are often lost or overlooked, so while you're assuming that your résumé has been received and reviewed and that they have declined you, they may not even know you exist. This is another reason why follow-up is so important. You may wind up needing to resubmit your résumé.

Fortunately, there are effective, professional ways of finding out if the company you're interested in has received your résumé. Finding out presents an opportunity for you to restate your desire to pursue the position and remind them of your qualifications and why you are the ideal person for the job.

WHOM SHOULD I CALL? Figuring out whom you should call is just as important as making the follow-up connection. You will have to identify the hiring manager responsible for screening and select-ing prospective candidates for the position. If it's a small company, you can usually call the main number and ask anyone who answers to provide you with the name of and contact information for the ap-propriate person. The larger the employer, the more complicated it often becomes to pinpoint the appropriate person. Among the op-tions:

1. Call the main number and ask to be connected to human re-sources. Sometimes an assistant will answer, and you'll be able to ask for the name of the person you're trying to reach. Always ask for the name of the assistant and create a connec-tion with him or her by expressing your gratitude. You can also ask for advice on the best time to try to reach the person you want to contact.

2. Visit the careers or jobs section of the company Web site to look for contact names and/or e-mail addresses and phone numbers. Some employers list this information by department or region.

3. Look at corporate press releases or a listing of top executives on the company Web site to determine who is the head of the division that interests you. (For public companies this infor-mation can be found on hoovers.com.) When you call the main switchboard, ask to be connected to that person's office. When an assistant answers, politely ask if she or he would kindly tell you who is responsible for recruiting for positions in the line of business you're pursuing. For example, if the position you're seeking is account manager in the consumer-products division, ask who handles that recruitment responsi-

bility. You do not have to identify yourself as a job seeker unless asked.

4. Ask a current employee to find out for you the name of the human-resources person you should connect with.

PERSISTENCE PAYS. Once you have a name, make this follow-up phone call a week after submitting your résumé. If the ad or posting stipulates "No phone calls, please," follow up using another communication method, such as e-mail. However, keep in mind that such rules are typically designed to ward off people who would ordinarily call up just to ask, "Have you received my résumé"—a question no human-resources professional has the time or desire to address.

When you're ready to pick up the phone, keep in mind that you have a dual purpose: to confirm that your résumé has been received and to further your candidacy by making a strong connection and impression. For example, "Hi, Ms. Goldman. My name is Haley Revez. Last week I submitted my résumé for the position of technical analyst. I'm following up with you now because I'd welcome the opportunity to discuss my qualifications." Before sharing additional information, pause briefly to allow her to acknowledge receipt of your résumé. If you have exceptional experience that makes you a standout candidate for this position, mention it here. In such a case, you'd say, "Hi, Ms. Goldman. My name is Haley Revez. I submitted my résumé last week for the position of technical analyst. You may have noticed my previous experience at Microsoft. Would you consider setting up an interview with me?" If she hasn't previously looked at the résumés submitted, or if yours was somehow overlooked, this additional information will likely cause her to pay attention.

If she says she doesn't recall seeing it or hasn't had a chance to check on what's been submitted, you may offer to send another copy. "I'm sure you've received many résumés for this posting. If it would be helpful to you, I'd be happy to e-mail another copy directly to your attention, especially since I meet and exceed all of the criteria outlined and I'd be ideal for the role."

If your initial statement prompts the response that your résumé has been received, you can say, "Great, I'm glad to know you received it so quickly. I was happy to hear that position was open, since I was an analyst in Chicago for six years and know a lot about your company. I also wanted to let you know I managed the XYZ project, which was delivered on time and under budget for the company." You may then ask what the next steps are in the hiring process and when a decision to fill the position is likely to be made. The goal is to not end the call until you have some sense of the time frame and the next steps. Is there someone else you should follow up with? Can you set up an interview now that you're on the phone? When might someone call you for an interview? Try to get a definite response as to what should happen next.

Resist the urge to leave a voice-mail message with your initial question. It is doubtful that your call will be returned. Keep trying until you get a live person on the line, which might mean varying the times of day at which you place your calls. Early morning, lunchtime, and end of work are the best times to try reaching key contacts in their offices.

WHERE DO I GO FROM HERE? The response you receive from this contact should determine if and when you get a callback, or when you should call again. If they seem irritated, you can apologize and back off. "I recognize that you're busy and that you've no doubt received many résumés for the position. What would be an appropriate way to follow up?" Be grateful and try your best to connect with that person, but don't persist by sharing details about your interest. Ask if there's a better time for you to call or if your inquiry should be directed to someone else. If, however, the contact person seems neutral or the least bit interested, keep on course until your message has been delivered. In the end, contact has been made, your interest has been reiterated, additional information has been supplied, and a request for a decision on next steps has been made.

If you have not heard anything after three weeks, follow up again, either with a call or an e-mail. Restate your desire for an interview. You don't want to spoil your chances by contacting the potential employer too often, but you don't want to be forgotten or overlooked either. There is a fine line between positive persistence and annoying pestering, but by combining common sense with these suggested procedures, you will greatly increase your chances for going from résumé submission to interview.

BETTER LUCK NEXT TIME. Let's say you did everything you were supposed to, from submitting your résumé to checking up on it at each stage, only to hear that you were not chosen for an interview. If it's a company you want to have a future opportunity with, and you want to learn where you went wrong or what you can do differently next time, ask. "I'm sorry to hear that news, but thank you for taking the time to consider me. In your professional opinion, is there anything I could do differently to better my chances with your company in the future?" Or you could say, "Was there anything pertaining to my experience or specific skills or knowledge that I could improve upon in order to increase my chances of employment at your company, since I'm eager to join your team?" Anything you can do to find out ways to improve your résumé and experience will help you in future job searches.

Additionally, if you didn't get to interview for this specific opening, ask if you can have a 15-minute information interview, which will allow you to find out more about the company and its hiring needs, as well as what makes a successful candidate. It will also allow you to tell your interviewer about your skills, experience, and achievements. This may cause her to recommend you for a future position. The goal is to stay in touch and follow up, since the person they hire might not work out or they might have a need for another employee before you know it.

How to Ask Smart Questions During an Interview to Help You Land the Job

Most people prepare for an interview by anticipating the questions they'll be asked—and practicing their answers. But what happens when the tables are turned and the interviewers ask if you have any questions for *them*. Consider asking questions that are specific to the company. You might concentrate on asking about the challenges it faces and its position within the industry in which it operates. Beyond those specifics, there are five more questions that you must be prepared to ask in any interview. These may provide you with valuable insight and further support your candidacy.

WHAT ARE THE BIGGEST CHALLENGES YOU SEE IN THIS POSITION? This shows an interviewer that you're interested in going beyond the basics and that you are inquisitive and thoughtful. It also shows that you're not adverse to overcoming challenges and tackling them with gusto. An interviewer will often reveal information that would otherwise have been difficult to ascertain. For example, he might let you know about specific projects that you'll be expected to tackle. Or she could let on that the various personalities in a specific division are difficult to work with. Whatever the response, you can use that information to address how you're ideally suited to rise to the occasion and handle those issues.

WHAT ARE YOU LOOKING FOR THE IDEAL CANDIDATE TO ACCOMPLISH IN THE FIRST SIX MONTHS? By asking this question, you're showing the interviewer that you are a results-oriented professional. All employers want goal-driven and motivated people on their teams. You're ready to hit the ground running with an eye toward accomplishing whatever is most important to your new employer. Finding out what an employer values and the expectations she or he has for this job candidate will help put both sides on the same page. It's beneficial to communicate your awareness of expectations and to make clear that you're willing and able to meet them.

WHY IS THIS POSITION VACANT? The answer might be either benign or a big eye-opener. The position might be new, which is great news because it likely means the company or division is growing. Someone might have been promoted, which is also positive because it's typically a sign that the company promotes from within. At other times the interviewer might let slip that they've had difficulty keeping someone because the manager is demanding and often difficult to work with. You'll want to know as much as possible, so take the opportunity to learn about what you might be stepping into in terms of culture and personalities.

WHAT ARE THE NEXT STEPS IN THE INTERVIEW PROCESS? Most interviewees make the mistake of leaving the interview without a sense of what to expect next. Ask this key question while you still have the attention of the interviewer. Find out if you'll have to meet with more people, agree to any kind of skill-based or psychological testing, or submit to drug tests and background checks. You should also ask if other people are being considered for the position, and where the company is in the hiring process. Be sure to inquire as to when you can expect to hear from someone about the next steps. Offer to call your contact in an agreed-upon time frame. The more you can glean from these answers, the less chance you will become frantic or frustrated because of uncertainty.

WHEN DO YOU EXPECT TO MAKE A DECISION? This question differs from the questions you'll be asking about the next steps in the process. You want to know their time frame for making a formal offer. You might learn that the company doesn't expect to make an offer for two to three months. Other times the period might be as short as a day or a week. The benefit of knowing their time frame is important in terms of managing your own needs and expectations. You'll also want to figure out who the final decision maker is, so that you will be prepared when interacting with that person.

In addition, it is advisable to ask about the company culture. You can say, "I know that you must determine if I'd be a good fit for your culture. Similarly, I want to make sure that this is a good match for me. I have a few questions about the philosophy and practices of the company that I hope you won't mind addressing." Among the questions you might want to ask:

- What is the policy for promoting from within?

- What is the turnover in the department I'm interviewing for? How does that compare with the turnover in the company as a whole?

- How would you describe the senior management style?

- How did you get your job here? Would you share your experience and impressions of the company with me?

By asking questions that show clear insight into the company's initiatives and goals, you are demonstrating to a potential employer that you will fit right in, that you understand their workplace culture, and that you are ready to go to work.

How to Ask for More Money

Some employers have no wiggle room, especially if the position has a fixed salary. This is common in entry-level training jobs. However, for more-typical positions, don't be agreeable to the first number just to get your foot in the door, especially since most employers actually expect that a successful candidate will ask for more money than what's being offered.

Men are four times more likely than women to negotiate the first offer; thus, they accumulate an average of a half-million dollars more in their paychecks by age 60. Whether by nature or nurture, many women shy away from negotiating salary. We assume that if we jump into the job, roll up our sleeves, and get down to business, someone

She Asked for It!

When I was a junior faculty member in a department of OB-GYN, there were five faculty members—four of whom were men, plus me—in the department available to take night call. Each person was assigned to take one day a week. I was assigned Friday, which meant that I would have to work every Friday night until eight on Saturday morning. This obviously spoiled any possible weekend plans every weekend.

I approached the department chairman, pointed out the problem with the schedule, and suggested that we either take call a week at a time or rotate Fridays so that no one would have every weekend spoiled. His response was that if I wanted to plan something on a weekend, I could ask someone to cover the call, but otherwise I still had to work every Friday.

This was a no-win situation, and I don't think there was anything that could have changed the outcome. It shows that not all work environments are fair or user-friendly for women. I suggest that in job interviews you keep your eyes open for corporate cultures that may be biased and avoid them if possible. There are better places to be, so why start out in a place where everything is an uphill battle? It doesn't have to be that way, and when it starts out bad, it frequently doesn't get better.

—DR. CARLENE ELSNER, reproductive endocrinologist and infertility specialist will notice us and reward us accordingly. Rarely does that happen, and so you wind up cheating yourself out of money by not asking for it.

Before you can ask for what you deserve, you have to make the commitment to negotiate. You must be willing to speak up and argue your worth by demonstrating the value you are bringing to your new employer.

No matter how excited you are, don't say yes immediately. Always assume the first offer is negotiable unless you've been told otherwise. Ask for the offer in writing, and take at least 24 to 48 hours to think it over; this "waiting period" offers breathing room to allow for other interviews if you have them. Make sure that you are clear about when you'll be getting back to them and that the time is acceptable to them.

Prior to discussing or negotiating a number that you'll be comfortable with, do your homework as to what the market is paying for someone with your skills. Figure out what comparable positions pay based on industry, level of experience, education, and geography. Check Department of Labor statistics and survey sites such as salary .com. Also look into industry-specific trade associations, which often track such data.

While it's okay to ask friends and colleagues in your field about their salaries, keep in mind that such responses are often inflated and can give you a false sense of reality. For example, approach knowledgeable peers by saying, "I don't want to appear to be prying, but I'm in the process of a salary negotiation, and I'd welcome your input on ranges that would be consistent with the going rates in this line of work." Or ask if there's someone they know in a related field whom you might call.

As you prepare to negotiate with a current or future employer, do the following:

FOCUS ON YOUR PERFORMANCE. The amount you are going to ask for shouldn't be based on your rent, car payments, babysitting needs, or other personal expenses. Mentioning those expenses will not make you more attractive to a company. Instead, focus on work: the demands of the position, your past and future responsibilities, your track record of success, and what the industry typically pays for such a position.

REMOVE THE EMOTION. Women often equate taking less money and not rocking the boat with being better-liked. Take the emotion out of the conversation. In an effective negotiation, your focus should be on receiving fair compensation for your work. You're asking for more money because you're smart, capable, and competent, not because you want someone to like you as a friend.

BE DIRECT ABOUT YOUR EXPECTATIONS. "Thank you for extending an offer. I'm excited about the possibility of joining your team. I've researched the industry, and people with skills and experience comparable to mine are earning an average of $45,000. That's $5,000 more than you're offering, so I'd like you to consider increasing the offer. Can you make this happen?"

Another example: "Is your offer of $45,000 in line with what others in the organization in the same position are making? I'm asking because the figure is lower than I anticipated."

You can also offer a range. "While I appreciate your offer and I know I'd be an exceptional asset to the company, I was expecting to earn between $45,000 and $50,000."

If you are moving to an area where the cost of living is higher, ask if a cost-of-living adjustment has been offered. "I realize that in my previous position in Salt Lake City, I was earning $35,000, but since this new opportunity is in Chicago, I would expect to earn at least $10,000 more."

If the offer is significantly less than you expected, let them know. "As I've said all along, I'm very interested in the position. However, I would not be able to accept it for $45,000, based on my qualifications as well as the challenges of the role. Would you reconsider?" Be prepared to hear them either say no because the offer is firm or ask what you have in mind.

ANTICIPATE THE OPPOSITION. Try figuring out in advance why your request might be rejected, and rehearse your responses. The more you play devil's advocate, the better prepared you'll be in the long run.

For example, when you ask for $10,000 more in base pay, your prospective employer might reject that figure, citing your low salary history. In such an instance, you can say, "I'm asking for this increase based on the skills and experience I bring to the position, as well as my track record of successes. There are significant challenges that I'll be expected to tackle in this new role, and my overall responsibilities will be much greater than in my previous positions. Therefore, I'm confident that the results I will achieve warrant this increase."

When asking for more money, don't make threats that you aren't willing to keep. Be prepared for the recruiter or human-resources person to show you the door if you give an ultimatum.

ESTABLISH ALTERNATIVES. Decide on your own in advance the least amount of money you'd be willing to take to accept the position. Then figure out what alternatives to your ideal salary are important to you. For example, $15,000 more might be tops on your list, but if the company won't budge on base salary, perhaps you can ask for a signing bonus, which often comes from a different budget. Your priority might be an extra week of vacation or a better title. Maybe you'd like to work from home one day a week or maintain a somewhat flexible schedule. Sometimes you can negotiate commuting or parking expenses as well.

You would ask for such alternatives by saying, for example, "Since you're unable to increase the base pay you offered me, I'd like to propose an extra week of vacation time. In my previous position, which I held for five years, I was eligible for three weeks, so I'm hoping you'll grant me the same amount of time here."

Consider walking away from the offer. Decide in advance what you'll do if your requests are rejected and the employer's offer is firm. Would you prefer to pass on the job offer and continue searching for a better opportunity? Or will you accept the offer as presented, with the satisfaction of knowing that you asked for what you deserved even though you didn't get it? It's essential to make this decision before negotiating.

THE BIG DAY. Rehearse your talking points in advance by role-playing with a confidante who can be an effective devil's advocate. When the time comes for the actual negotiation, whether it is by phone or in person, bring bulleted notes that reinforce your key points.

PROFESSIONAL FOLLOW-UP. In the end, the company may still decline your offer. Be proud that you stood firm, and keep your cool even in the face of rejection. If they say no to your requests and you're unwilling to budge, send a genuine note of thanks within two days after the decision has been made. This leaves a positive professional impression, and might even result in a callback with a counteroffer. Keep the door open by letting the decision maker know that perhaps you'll have the opportunity to work together in the future.

CELEBRATE YOURSELF. When you are one of the deserving women who does get the salary you asked for and you're proud of it, be careful not to boast to your coworkers. Project your confidence and satisfaction from knowing that you asked for and received what you wanted and deserved, but don't become the Shelly Show-off of the office, whom no one can bear to be around. Tact and discretion will keep you out of trouble.

How to Ask About Compensation and Benefits

Base salary isn't the only important aspect of the job offer. Many women either ignore or are unaware of the numerous options available to them; they focus on the salary only, which is a big mistake. There are a few important things to ask about once you've been offered the position:

- Be direct and ask about the overall compensation package by saying, "Since salary is just part of the overall compensation, it is important for me to know about the whole benefits package available to employees. Is there a package you could share with me?" When possible, get this in writing so that you can review the benefits and fully evaluate the offer. Your prospective employer has no doubt invested a lot of time and money in developing its benefits plan, so ask questions whose answers will give you a direct and complete understanding of what's available to you.

- Ask about specific benefits, including insurance — medical, dental, vision, disability, and life-insurance coverage. You should ask what plans the employer offers, as well as what portion of the monthly premium(s) the employer contributes and when you become eligible for it. Also ask what is the minimum number of work hours required for eligibility, and if your spouse, domestic partner, or children are also eligible for coverage. If your previous employer paid your premium in full each month while your new employer pays none of it, then you might be getting a pay *decrease*, not an *increase*.

- Be aware of the different types of health coverage available versus what your employer may offer: traditional (fee-for-service), HMO (health-maintenance organization), and PPO (preferred-provider organization). Read over your options to help you decide which plan will meet your needs. Consider a variety of situations and what-ifs and educate yourself about what these plans really mean. What are your deductibles? What will you owe at appointments? Are there additional benefits that provide emotional security as well? The fine print often reveals these details, and it's important to understand in full what you are being offered.

MORE COMPENSATION. What about other benefits that may be available to you, like paid time off (PTO), vacation days, sick days, and personal days? How are they accrued? What are the specific terms? Can the unused time be carried over to the next year, or must it be used by a certain date? Does the company offer domestic-partner benefits? Are bereavement days covered? If so, what is the policy? If you're not pregnant now, but might consider becoming pregnant at some point during your employment at this new company, ask up front what type of coverage is offered just so you're totally clear.

You can ask about other types of paid or unpaid leave. These might include sabbaticals after a certain number of years of continuous service.

Long- or short-term disability, severance packages, or company takeovers: Companies are not required to offer benefits to protect you in these cases, but you should definitely ask about them so that you'll be prepared. You might want to ask about notice periods in case your position is eliminated. This information can often be found in an employment agreement.

Retirement plans—401k plans: In most of these cases the employee and employer contribute money to the account via automatic payroll deductions. Ask how much you will be able to contribute and what, if any, match the employer offers. Ask when you can begin to contribute to the plan, when the matching component (if any) begins, and what the vesting schedule is for the matched amounts.

Stock options: Ask if there are any stock programs available for employees. Depending on the options, you may want to consult your own financial planner, accountant, or stockbroker to determine the best options for participation. Even with a small start-up, profit-sharing and stock options could be valuable to you. Think of the early Google guys who are now seeing huge dollar signs and early retirement because of their stock compensation.

If the person you are negotiating with can't answer your questions in detail, ask to speak to someone in the corporate-benefits department who is likely to be more familiar with the information you're requesting. Ask to see a copy of the employee handbook or corporate-benefits summary. Ask to see a total-compensation statement so that you can understand what your total package will be worth, not just the portion that you receive in a paycheck.

OTHER BENEFITS YOU MIGHT WANT TO INQUIRE ABOUT.

Expense Account: Depending on your position and level of experience, you may be eligible for this. "Is there an expense account that comes with my position for entertaining clients, vendors, or suppliers? What is the procedure for being reimbursed when I purchase items for business use?"

Child care assistance: Is it available? Is it offered on a daily basis, or is it reserved for emergency and backup occasions? What are the costs, and what ages are admitted?

Elder care assistance: Is it available? And if so, what are the specific services or referral programs?

Telecommuting: Is it a possibility for this position? What expenses are covered if we agree to this option? Do you provide a computer, phone, internet access, or other aids?

Educational support: Is there a tuition-reimbursement policy for continuing education or degrees? How many classes per semester or year are reimbursed? Are fees and books covered? When does an employee become eligible? Are there any stipulations, such as certain grades or approved courses, for reimbursement?

Employee-assistance programs (EAPs): Since many employers recognize the need for resources that address a myriad of personal issues, ask if you'd have access to any confidential referral services. These programs might focus on such challenges as mental illness, family disagreements, substance abuse, divorce, and financial pressures.

Health and wellness: Does the company offer discounted membership to a local gym, or do they have an on-site fitness center for employees? Is there a subsidized cafeteria? Some companies even offer daily aerobic breaks right in the office—a few minutes of daily stretching and movement can be the little extra nudge you need to a healthier, happier lifestyle and career.

Other programs: Healthcare-reimbursement accounts, which allow for pretax deductions on unreimbursed health-related expenses; transportation savings accounts, which provide for the purchase of vouchers for commuting, using pretax dollars; college scholarships, grants, or savings plans for your dependents' higher education; purchase plans for discounted rates on big-ticket products or services offered by the employer; and concierge services, including the procurement of theater tickets, on-site dry cleaning, car washing, and other services of convenience.

While you don't have to grill the human resources department on every detail prior to accepting an offer, use your judgement to determine which benefits are valuable and relevant to you.

She Asked for It!

The first company I worked for closed down. When I was offered an ideal position with a lower salary, I didn't think I was in a position to negotiate. I knew that the long-term benefits from a financial and quality-of-work perspective would be very rewarding. I was able to convince the company to grant me more stock options as I believed the company had a solid product and future. I negotiated an additional 1,000 options to my package.

—SANDRA KRIEF, Senior System Engineer

How to Ask for Time Off Before Accepting a Position

During the interview process, there may be important dates on your mind that will likely conflict with your new position if you wind up receiving a formal offer. It could be a long-standing vacation, a wedding, surgery, or another important event to which you had a prior commitment.

Don't wait until you've accepted the job to ask for the necessary time off. Instead, do it in the final stages of the negotiation process, after it's been made clear that the company wants you.

YOU'VE BEEN OFFERED THE POSITION. Once you have been offered the job and you know you want to accept it, ask for the time off as part of the deal. "Thank you for the offer. I'm very excited about joining the team. I know there will be time to discuss all the details, but I wanted to let you know upfront that I will need the last week of May off for a long-standing commitment that I cannot break. Will that be an issue? I'd like to discuss in advance how to work that into my paid time off."

Here is an approach for another situation: "My family and I have planned our summer vacation a year in advance, and I don't want to miss it. Not only would I lose our substantial deposit and airfare, but I'd disappoint the kids as well. I want to accept your offer for this position; however, I need your assurance that this trip will not be jeopardized. Will that be an issue?"

ESTABLISH ALTERNATIVES. An alternative is offering to make up the days off. For example: "During the first two days of June, I have a prior engagement that I committed to before beginning this interview process. Would I be able to take those days off with pay, and make up for them by staying later or working on a weekend?"

One condition you could make for accepting the position could be the employer's willingness to extend those days off to you, even if your vacation wouldn't typically kick in that soon. Do not volunteer to take the time off unpaid, but you should keep in mind that you may ultimately have to do so if they won't budge on their policy. This should be a last resort on your part. Once you receive approval, put it in writing so that it doesn't fall between the cracks.

When negotiating time off, you may need to give up something to achieve it. For example, you might ask by saying, "I appreciate the one week of vacation starting in six months. Would I be able to take an additional week off unpaid if I took my vacation during a slow time for the company?" Be prepared to have to prove yourself before such a request is granted. Results and performance are the drivers for getting special privileges.

How to Ask About a Position's Salary Without Divulging Your Salary History

Your goal is to discover what a company is willing to pay for a position, but you want to do so without discussing your past salary, and without selling yourself short or knocking yourself out of the ballpark.

RESEARCH NUMBERS. Find out the market value of your position. Sites like vault.com offer insights into specific companies' salaries via message boards and white papers. If it's a government position, the pay range may be published in the posting. If you want to do general research, you can do this through salary.com and industry-specific associations that track salaries in particular areas of interest and geography.

If you're changing careers or entering a different field, expect a different salary range, since you may not have all the qualifications the position requires. Alternatively, if you're going from a nonprofit to a for-profit organization, or if you're moving from a small city to a big one, you don't want your smaller salary to be taken for lack of ability. Keep this in mind as you are inquiring about or researching compensation. Be practical, yet have confidence in what you can offer your future employer now and after you've been hired.

When initially inquiring about a position—over the phone, in person, or via e-mail—you can ask the person handling your inquiry,

"What is the general salary range for this position?" Don't dance around the issue. Get right to it. This way you'll know if it's worth your time going through the rest of the process. If they won't respond with a specific answer, ask for a range. Some people are not forthcoming with information, but usually they'll provide what you need if you ask directly.

DO YOU HAVE TO TELL THEM? This is a tricky one. Some companies claim they can't and won't decide what you're worth if they don't know your entire salary history, yet most job seekers feel that it's confidential information.

Other employers have suggested they don't need an exhaustive list of past salaries, but they would like to know your most recent earnings to determine if you're in the right ballpark for this new opportunity.

When you are filling out applications and encounter the salary-history area, do not leave it blank. Complete it honestly; otherwise, you may ruin your chances of even being considered for the position. Remember that before hiring you, most employers will insist on verifying this information, either by calling your former employer(s) or requesting the previous years' W-2s for proof. If you've lied, this is the time you will be busted and lose the offer.

THE INTERVIEW. If you've come this far and still haven't learned or been told of the position's salary, try to avoid questions about money until you've learned more about the position from the interviewer. There could be more to the job—good and bad—than you know at this point, and you don't want to come across as if salary was the only thing on your mind. Say, "I'd like to hear more about the position before talking about salary," or, "First I had a question about . . ." (whatever is also important to you at that time in the interview). This will impress the interviewer by showing your interest, and the additional information will provide you with more power when the time to negotiate finally comes.

Either way, be prepared if the interviewer asks you to provide your past salary history. You can reply politely and directly, "I'm very interested in this position and your company. While I can be somewhat flexible on salary if the opportunity is right, it would help me to know the general range that you're able to offer."

In the end, don't risk alienating or annoying a prospective employer with your unwillingness to answer the question. At some point, you're going to have to provide your information, just as you expect the company to provide a number as well. Be careful about dismissing a potential opportunity solely because of the base salary offered or advertised. Ultimately, you'll need to factor in the company, the people you'd be working with, the potential for growth, and your own goals. Collectively, some of that might be more important than the salary alone.

How to Ask About Next Steps in the Interview Process

Figuring out the next steps in any career-related process—whether applying for the job, interviewing for the position, or negotiating the offer—is your chance to manage your expectations and set the course to make things happen. If you don't get the critical details aligned, it's difficult to know what to expect and when, which often

She Asked for It!

I was negotiating salary for my first serious job. I was offered the money, and instead of taking it, I said, "Let me think about it," and I went to the ladies' room and cried. I went back and said I couldn't live with it. They then offered me more money, and I called my father, who said, "What, are you crazy? Take the money!" Once again, I didn't. So I went back in and asked one final time. They increased the offer, and I took it.

They didn't know I was upset, but I was crying because I had to ask, and it was hard to imagine a nice girl like me asking for money. In those days, you wanted them to give you money because they liked you and you were worth it. I learned that not only is there absolutely no shame in asking, but that they expect you to ask. You don't just get it because you're nice.

—DR. JUDITH SILLS, *clinical psychologist and author,*
The Comfort Trap: What If You're Riding a Dead Horse

means you won't make the most of an opportunity. Getting into the mind-set of asking requires planning and preparation. Here are some situations to be prepared for during the interview process:

NEXT-STEP SCENARIOS. If you meet a recruiter at a career expo and you discuss details about a specific opportunity, don't walk away without saying, "This sounds wonderful, and I'm so appreciative of your time. When and how should I follow up with you?" As with any question, watch your body language. If you are nervous—fumbling for your résumé or unable to find a pen—that minute-made impression will be lasting. Be confident; otherwise, you are sending a message that you are not prepared. It's also a good idea to ask for the contact's business card in order to make sure you have the correct spelling of her name and the right contact information. If she prefers for you to contact her by e-mail, then you'll have a record and her permission to do so.

Say you're at a holiday gathering and you strike up a conversation with a friend or family member, which leads to the discovery that he has a great contact for you. Don't wait for him to call you with the details, because he's certain to forget. Take the initiative after the event by saying, "I appreciated your mention of a possible contact at last night's dinner. I'm calling to see if I might get that name and number from you." Each of these situations demonstrates one key factor, which is follow-through. Many jobs and opportunities are lost due to dropping the ball and not taking action. Determining next steps is critical: it puts you back in charge and makes you feel empowered.

During an interview there are many questions you can ask that will help move things to the next steps:

"Will another interview be necessary? If so, with whom will I be interviewing?"

"What should I bring with me to our next session?"

"Are any tests required?"

"How many open positions do you have?"

"What is your timing on filling this position?"

Never leave an interview without establishing the next steps. "When should I expect to hear from someone?"

Alternatively, you can state when *you* will be contacting *them*. "Thanks again, Mr. Smyth. I'll follow up with a call in a few days to see where things stand. Would that be okay with you?"

The next steps are like closing in on a deal or sale. You want to move the process forward in order to get the job in the end. For this reason, treat every interview as if it were your last. Be nice to everyone, including the receptionist and other staffers with whom you are required to interact. Their impressions of you could help seal the deal or nix the offer.

AFTER THE INTERVIEW. Always send an e-mail or handwritten thank-you note to the person or people with whom you've interviewed. Be sure to also thank the person who set up the interview(s). All of the messages should be unique. Double-check your spelling and grammar. Do not send one form e-mail to everyone. Your notes should reiterate your desire to join the company. This is also a good time to cover anything you forgot to mention during the interview, such as additional qualifications, anecdotes, or recommendations. Include your contact information, such as a phone number where you can be reached; you can use a business card. Make it easy for someone to connect with you.

When it's time to place the follow-up call as you indicated you would, say something like, "Hello, Mr. Smyth. This is Maria Hernandez. I interviewed with you last week for the marketing-manager position, and, as you suggested, I'm touching base with you today to see where things stand in the hiring process."

NOT YET. If they haven't yet reached a decision, ask, "Would you please let me know if I am still a candidate for the position?" If you are, then you can add, "When would it be best for me to check back with you?" If you sense some hesitation on the part of the interviewer, you could say, "If there's any hesitancy about my candidacy, I hope you'll share it with me so that I can perhaps answer other questions or provide more information as to why I'd be a great asset." If you feel it's essential, you can also offer to work on a trial basis to prove yourself.

Continue with the weekly follow-up, or whatever timetable is most suitable based on the feedback you received. Be patient and polite, keeping in mind that decisions aren't often made according to our ideal time frames.

NO. If their answer to you is no, make sure you leave them with a positive impression. Since the potential for future opportunities could still exist, you don't want to jeopardize their opinion of you. Be gracious. "Even though this didn't work out as I had hoped, I am appreciative of your time and initial interest in me. And I hope you'll keep me in mind for future opportunities. In the meantime, I'd welcome any feedback as to what the selected candidate possessed that you didn't see in me. Perhaps there's something I can learn that will help me grow." And in case they were positive about your interview but had many other qualified candidates, and provided that you are still interested, consider dropping the contact a note letting him know you are still available should there be another related opening.

YES. When you hear the news that they'd like to hire you, be calm and enthusiastic, but don't necessarily accept the offer just yet. There could exist the potential for negotiation. "That's terrific, I'm delighted by this news. If possible, I'd like to receive your offer in writing." Then ask, "What are the next steps in the process so that we can agree on the terms and my start date?"

She Asked for It!

Like any good job applicant, I had researched the finances of the organization. I was interviewing for the position of executive director of the Atlanta Press Club and was truly thrilled when offered the position. I believed it to be the perfect job for me, and it has turned out to be just that.

However, the first offer was considerably lower than what I had hoped for. I remember feeling confused and hurt and not quite knowing how to respond. Like many women, I took it personally. My husband turned out to be the perfect career coach. We researched salaries of comparable positions and did our best to determine what was reasonable for the Press Club and fair to me. I then made a counteroffer.

My husband convinced me to ask for exactly what I wanted and made me believe I was worth it. I thought it was a bold move and was afraid they would laugh in my face. They did just the opposite. I believe in retrospect that it raised their respect for me. I was able to say, "If you meet this salary requirement, I'm in." They did, and here I am.

—SARAH DOUGLAS, *executive director, Atlanta Press Club*

How to Ask to Be Considered for Positions
Outside of Stereotypical Roles

Not every position is going to put you on the fast track to the top. In fact, most support positions, which are traditionally held by women, rarely lead to advancement to the highest levels in a company. The roles that will help you reach the top are called line jobs. These positions directly impact the company's bottom line—its profits and losses.

Roles in public relations and human resources support line jobs. This is often true whether you work for a Fortune 500 corporation, a small nonprofit, or a midsize law firm. Rotating into jobs where you are responsible for revenue generation is essential when you want to reach the top level in an organization. Consider any number of line jobs: find the fun in finance, act as an accounting ace, sell with sizzle, or offer to optimize operations. See yourself as CEO, and become the boss.

Lack of information about various positions is a key reason why many women hit the proverbial glass ceiling. Not enough women are skilled at getting sufficient diverse experience inside their companies to allow them to attain the advancement they are seeking. The first step is to project where your current job experience will take you. Quite often, the pinnacle of your current path is easy to see. It may simply be department head.

The way out of this box is to start talking about your career goals with your supervisor early on. Don't begin this conversation by sharing pie-in-the-sky fantasies of being CEO. Instead, show a commitment to your boss, your department, and your current career path by sharing your desire to expand upon your *current* expertise. Say, "I'm very interested in building a long-term career with the company. What types of responsibilities tend to enhance a skill-set like mine?"

You may also identify someone in senior management who once worked in your department and say to your boss, "I've been impressed with Barbara's career. What additional skills did she develop to put her in line for senior management?" These conversations should stay focused on how you can acquire greater strength in your current job. Show loyalty with inquisitiveness.

IF YOU MEET WITH RESISTANCE. In some cases, your supervisor will be supportive and give you the information you want. Other times, however, you will be met with resistance. In situations like this, don't pursue the conversation with superiors in your department. Instead, consider asking someone outside of your department for advice. You can also look into company advancement programs on your own. Approach senior-management women inside and outside your organization and ask them how they developed their careers. Say, "I've really admired your career and understand that you once worked in investor relations. What additional skills did you need to acquire to attain your current position?"

HOW TO AVOID GETTING STUCK. Of course, not all women have built their careers in support roles. Many women work in line jobs like sales and consulting, and are subject to the same issues as those that women in staff jobs confront. Women in line jobs, admittedly, deal with these issues to a lesser extent. The issue here is that line jobs tend to have a narrow focus. Support positions often address the bigger picture. For this reason, women in line jobs also need to concern themselves with job rotation—at least once or twice in their careers. The risk, however, is getting stuck permanently in a support position. The best way to handle this is to develop your plan in writing so you're clear about your goals and how you will achieve them.

If you aren't able to rotate into other roles inside your company, consider a rotating out of the company altogether. Stay proactive and skillfully manage your career. Although women now make up half of the workforce, they are underrepresented in senior positions. Very few women currently make it to the top of their organization, but progress with advancement is underway.

The numbers are moving in the right direction, however, with an increasing number of female corporate officers in the Fortune 500 over the past decade. Women at this level help set the policy that affects the rest of the workforce. You will find that your experiences at work will be enhanced as more women reach these pinnacles. And who says you can't be the next Meg Whitman or Andrea Jung? The workforce needs smart women—women like you—in executive positions.

How to Ask for a Paid Internship

You are now ready to take your classroom knowledge and acquire professional skills in a specific field. An internship will help you accomplish that goal. It will also strengthen your résumé and create connections you can use down the road. Although paid internships are not common in all fields, there are ways to get them.

Companies are investing more time in and devoting more resources to internship programs because they can often lead to the identification and grooming of future employees. Most of the leading entertainment and publishing companies do not have paid internships, since there are so many people who want to be interns in these enterprises. The big businesses of investment banking, accounting, and technology have the best-paid internship programs. Compensation will vary according to region, company, and even size of employer.

There are many people to ask for help with regard to landing a paid internship. You can approach professors, college career counselors, and friends and family for their suggestions. "I'm interested in pursuing a paid internship this summer where I can apply my engineering skills. Would you have suggestions about small- to-medium-sized employers that I might look into about this?"

Although your focus will be hands-on education rather than employment, you should search for the right internship in the same way that you would search for a permanent job. This internship could lead to valuable recommendations for future employment, or you might be the one intern they don't want to get away. Research potential organizations, choose a program or customize one of your own, and then do your evaluations. Remember, you can do an internship almost anywhere in the world if you can afford to do so.

Ask yourself what skills you want to gain from this position. What knowledge would you bring to an employer? Are there any restrictions you have during the internship, such as number of hours you're available to work, or transportation or housing needs? Once you apply, be prepared to interview either by phone or in person. Consider the talents you bring to work and be prepared to address a variety of questions. The interviewer may ask:

"What are your plans after graduation?"

"How did you become interested in this field?"

"How have your courses prepared you for this internship?"

"What are your goals in relation to a possible internship here?"

"Why did you choose us?"

"What are your strengths?"

"What are your weaknesses?"

Be ready to ask questions in return:

"What will be my responsibilities?"

"Who would be my supervisor, and what are his expectations from interns?"

"Do you offer any type of intern training?"

"Have you hired any of your former interns in full-time positions?"

"At the end of my internship, assuming you're pleased with my performance, would you be willing to write me a recommendation and review my résumé?"

When it's time to discuss the important subject of compensation, you could say, "While I know this internship will offer me invaluable experience, for which I am very grateful, I am hoping you'll consider providing a stipend. Is that possible?"

Alternatively, you can focus on extra hours and the unique skills that you bring to the position. "Since I have expenses associated with accepting this internship, I'd like to respectfully request that you consider providing some compensation based on the long hours I'll put in and the special skills that I'll be bringing to this position. For example, I interned at another leading public-relations firm last semester and personally cultivated many media contacts who will take my calls. Secondly, I belong to the local press club and public-relations society as well as the networking group in this area. I would be delighted to network on your company's behalf, identifying potential clients."

Keep in mind that you will probably have more room for negotiation with a small company than with a large one. This is because bigger companies have formal internship programs that involve hundreds of positions annually. Some provide stipends while others do not, and some of these companies actually post this information. It's rare for them to make an exception in order to compensate one person.

If your request is rejected, which might very well be the case if there's a standard internship program and deviations are not permitted, then you might suggest being reimbursed for your travel, lunch expenses, or even a particular professional organization that you'd like to join in order to help the the company. Even though you won't make any money on the internship, this would prevent it from costing you money. On rare occasions there is such a thing as a free lunch, and as a starving college student, you deserve it.

Before you reject an unpaid position, keep in mind the long-term benefits of an unpaid internship in your field versus a paid hourly position outside of your industry of choice. For example, indirect compensation such as discounts on services or products, and attending seminars and participating in training workshops, can be very beneficial to your professional growth. It might also be possible to negotiate an internship that is unpaid for the first half and then paid in the second half. To determine if this is possible, ask if other interns have ever been hired on this basis. Also, inquire if you will be allowed to list specific assignments you did for the company's clients on your résumé under your internship credit. At the very least, will the company give you a letter of recommendation if you do a great job? Other benefits are likely to increase your career opportunities and salary down the road. You can view these rewards as delayed compensation. Take into consideration that:

- You will end your college or graduate school career with exceptional work experience.

- You will have benefited from real-world instruction.

- You may have earned college credit toward your major.

- You will have made important networking contacts.

- You will have gained hands-on experience in your field of choice, which may further your interest in that field or prove that you're no longer interested in it.

How to Ask for a Temporary Assignment

Are you ready to launch a career without any prior work experience? Maybe you can't decide on a specific career field just yet. It's okay if you're still test-driving in many areas of your life—be it cars, homes, clothing, partners, or your career path. Take the time to find your right match. What if you're between jobs and just need to make some extra income and keep your skills sharp? Temporary assignments are a great way to gain these experiences while also bringing in some extra spending money.

You can suggest a temporary assignment when a company doesn't have an available opening or they can't afford you on an annual basis. Typically, no benefits are provided, and there's no guarantee of long-term employment, but you often can make more money per hour or per day than you would if you were a salaried employee.

When you meet with the decision maker, say something like, "I'm very interested in this position, and I know I have a lot to offer your team. Since you don't have the ability to hire me full-time, would you consider a temporary assignment?"

Another scenario is, "The human-resources manager informed me that your receptionist is on maternity leave. I'm in between jobs and have great experience and references in customer service. I'd love to talk to you about hiring me temporarily for that position. This would provide you a wonderful opportunity to meet your current needs, while we could also see if we are a good fit going forward."

The majority of people in long-term temporary assignments are offered full-time positions. Businesses often find themselves in rough spots where there is a need to fill in for staff members who have quit or retired or are vacationing. The assignments can range from one day to a year, depending on the positions. And there will often be positions that require people with much flexibility. Show off your ability to adjust, negotiate, and problem-solve. You and your superiors will respect you for it.

For temporary assignments, you must have the kind of personality, skills, and great attitude that allow you to quickly adapt to new surroundings and new people. If you do, the possibilities are endless. It's exciting, and you'll gain insights into other businesses, along with training and connections. In all cases, you may need to go through the usual interview process, which will focus on your skills and interests. You may also need to take tests that pertain to the position.

However, the turnaround time for hiring is often much shorter than with a full-time staff position, which is welcome news.

It's a smart solution if you can't decide which career path to choose. Temping is the ultimate job-hunting strategy. You can experience the job behind the scenes without having to commit to a company and/or position full-time or permanently unless you choose to do so. It's a win-win situation all around and allows you the opportunity to see where you best fit and what type of job or work culture you might want to pursue once you decide you want permanent employment.

Temp assignments provide flexibility, allowing you to personalize your schedule to fit the needs of your lifestyle, the demands of the assignments, and the vision of the company.

The employer may also provide competitive compensation. Again, wages will vary with each company, but they often match or exceed the hourly rate of the equivalent full-time position.

You could sign up for Temp-to-Direct hire: it is a great alternative to looking before you leap and is good for both you and the employer, because there's less pressure on both of you. Hopefully you'll fall in love with the opportunity, and the employer won't be able to do without you and will end up hiring you directly.

How to Ask for a Meeting with a CEO

Despite what some people think is conventional wisdom, contacting the CEO should be the last resort when you are looking to break into a company. Every day thousands of people call, e-mail, and write asking to see the big boss. And while the "I've got nothing to lose" mentality is often accurate, if the majority of these meetings were granted, CEOs would never be able to run their companies and satisfy their shareholders.

If you're trying to reach the CEO of a small or medium-sized business, it's definitely worth a shot to call the main number and ask for the e-mail address or fax number of the top executive. You might even get the person on the phone easily, in which case, go for it by stating your request as quickly and succinctly as possible. "I've admired your company and followed its growth for the last year. I have a brilliant marketing idea that is tailor-made for you. Would you consider giving me 10 minutes to stop by and present it in person?"

When trying to connect with the CEO of a large company, there are several points of etiquette to guide your approach:

FOLLOW THE PROPER PROTOCOL. Many people attempt to e-mail the CEO directly, which rarely if ever secures a meeting, as the big boss doesn't usually see those letters. They're routed to an assistant, who is likely to be annoyed that you didn't follow the proper protocol of contacting her in the first place. Most people who wind up getting a meeting with a CEO are smart and savvy enough to go through the assistant whose job it is to handle all the CEO's scheduling decisions. You will have a better chance of receiving a positive response if you do the same.

LEVERAGE MUTUAL CONNECTIONS, BUT DON'T EXPECT FAVORITISM. It is to your advantage to write to the CEO via his or her assistant if you share a mutual connection. However, never lie or overstate the strength of that tie. There's a real chance that you'll get an interview if you have a strong résumé, but there's absolutely no guarantee that you'll get the job. The best companies won't hire you just because you know the boss or his cousins. Similarly, CEOs often bring in stacks of résumés from people they've met on the road or at speaking engagements, and all of them are typically directed to human resources with the caveat that there should not be any preferential treatment. Any good CEO wants his experts and leaders in each line of the business to make their own hiring decisions without unfair influence from the boss.

GO DIRECTLY TO THE RIGHT DEPARTMENT. It's usually more effective to go directly to the person who is specific to your needs. For example, if you have a terrific marketing proposal or you're looking for a marketing position, there are many people within the company's marketing division who've been empowered to make the needed decisions. If you're selling a product that you think is essential to a company's technical operations, go to the head of that department. This is not just good advice for salespeople and job seekers: when a mayor's office calls the CEO, they are often directed to the company's government-affairs group. It's not that the mayor isn't afforded respect, but there are people who are suited to handle those needs more effectively than the CEO. Rarely will the CEO of a major corporation override that team's authority to make decisions. He relies on their good judgment. Even when a CEO is approached by his own employees in the halls, he encourages them to take their good ideas to the proper manager.

TALK TO YOUR BOSS. Many internal employees want to impress the CEO with their ideas, especially when they believe they can transform a company. While there's nothing wrong with that, going to the boss is often not the most beneficial course of action. Think about speaking to your front-line supervisor, your manager, or your VP first. Often your own department has a better chance of making something happen—especially if the idea is valid. Start within your group, build some consensus, and then offer the idea to your department managers.

If you've exhausted the other possibilities and you're still convinced that you deserve time with the CEO, make sure your prior course of action is detailed in your request. That history will be important to the decision-making process of the person who will ultimately grant or deny your request.

SAVE YOUR MONEY. Gifts don't influence a CEO's decision to meet with you. Sending cookies or other gifts doesn't influence any large company's decision-making process and can be perceived as hokey. In cases where such stunts do work, it is because they are directly related to the field. For example, an advertising executive once granted a meeting to an employee who, to describe his focus, created an ad campaign that was so clever, the executive couldn't resist meeting with him. However, such tactics rarely work. If you're the creative type, just remember that the bar for success is high. In addition, with ethics issues in the forefront of the highest levels of management in most corporate cultures today, assistants and executives are more cautious than ever about showing favor based on the receipt of a gift. To get the attention of the CEO or his assistant, send a straightforward letter with no frills attached. It will surely garner more respect.

SOME SOFT SPOTS EXIST. Because companies value education, a student writing a paper who requests a few minutes with the CEO might receive a brief phone appointment to ask his or her questions. Many students don't know the ins and outs of a public-relations department, so students are sometimes excused from following the typical protocol. An adult businessperson is expected to understand the rules and follow them.

Remember, very few strangers receive in-person meetings with a CEO, so don't take a refusal personally. Meeting time is typically reserved for staff members reporting directly, members of the media, and external partners who are critical to the smooth operation of the company.

Executive assistants, especially those who support Fortune 100–level management, are often perceived as pit bulls because they are tough about who gets through, but it's their job to make sure the CEO's time is economized so that she or he can run the company as efficiently as possible.

How to Ask for More Time to Make Your Decision About an Offer

The day will come—maybe while you are in the middle of a project, or while you are switching jobs, or even while you are in an interview—when you'll need more time to make a decision. Without laying anything on the line, how do you delay answering the person in charge in order to give yourself ample time to decide what's best for you?

You've just been offered a job, but you really want to hear back from your interview from yesterday so that you can compare companies and salary packages before making your decision. You also might be interested in making a counteroffer. You know that if you ask for more time, the interviewer will expect to hear back from you in a day or two. If she doesn't, she just may retract the offer.

Thank her and buy time by saying, "I appreciate the offer, and I

She Asked for It!

I was bused to the Astrodome in Houston in the wake of Hurricane Katrina, and I was fearful about the future. When I saw a woman holding a sign that read ARE YOU LOOKING FOR A JOB?, I jumped up to get the chance to speak with her. I described my situation and she offered to help. The woman turned out to be Tory Johnson, and she kept her promise by finding me immediate employment and housing after this terrible disaster.

When I told other Katrina victims about my good fortune, they wondered how I was so lucky. I told them it wasn't just a matter of coincidence, I actually made my own luck by standing up and asking for help. I've learned that help rarely falls into our laps. You have to be willing to recognize that you need it, then you have to muster the confidence to ask for it. I'm thankful that I had the guts to ask for help.

—DORIS BANKS, *Houston Texas*

respect the fact that you usually need an answer in 24 hours, but I'd like to ask you to make an exception. I'm immersed in a project this week. Would you be able to give me a few days?" This demonstrates loyalty. Once you've made your decision, notify the person immediately via phone or in writing based on past communication.

Imagine being told that you were chosen as a contender for a transfer to the big city. It will mean not only a higher salary and a more prominent title, but a whole new life—and your interviewer wants an answer by Friday. You have a whole lot to think about, so it's not inappropriate to ask the employer to allow you time to consider the offer.

Immediately respond that because of the nature of the situation, you need time to think. "Off the bat, I'm delighted about the possibility of your offer; however, that's a significant decision to make, for which I'll need more than just a few days. I'd like more time to consider all aspects of what this might mean for me. What time frame would be acceptable to you?"

INTERNAL CHANGES. You work for a small company that you love. It's review time, and you're in a meeting with your boss. She informs you that the company is going through some rough waters and won't be able to grant you a raise. Worse, she asks you to take a pay cut, promising that when the company gets back on its feet, she will make it up to you. You might say, "While I'm aware that things have been tight, I'm very surprised to be asked to take a pay cut. I've delivered solid results above and beyond what's required of me. [Pause to breathe.] Of course, I value my position and would hate to consider the idea of looking elsewhere for work. But wouldn't you agree that I deserve a week or so to get my thoughts in order?" To have the benefit of the full picture, you should also ask if pay cuts are being made across the board. While you're buying more time to make your decision, consider asking for benefits to compensate for the possible cut, and develop a time line that shows when your pay would increase.

METHODS FOR DECISION MAKING.

- Allow the news to soak in. Your mind is trying to digest reality right now. Let it. Take a bath, go for a jog, or listen to music to relax you and help you consider the options with a clear head.

- Evaluate your options. You have the power to accept or decline the offer. Consider all sides of the equation based on the short- and long-term implications. Don't focus on pleasing others; focus on doing what's best for you.

- Weigh the pros and the cons of your options by using cost-benefit analysis. Make a list, and assign a value to each: pros (0 to +10), cons (0 to −10). Add the totals up for each and compare the outcomes. This is a great way to gain a better perspective. Bounce your thoughts off a family member or trusted friend.

- Get some sleep. Many problems are solved this way. As you're falling asleep, think about your situation, the choices you have, your feelings about each of them, and the possible results. Maybe you'll have your answer in the morning.

- When you make your decision, stand by it, and don't look back. Throw yourself into your decision and commit all of yourself.

If your boss doesn't grant you the extra time you request, let the issue be for the moment. Go back to your office and take a break. Even an hour or a day can bring about change, whereby the boss might be willing to give you a bit more time, and you might be willing to take a bit less time. If you're being pressed for an instant response, try providing one or two valid reasons why it's beneficial for both sides that you have this time. For example, it will ensure that you make the best decision for yourself and the company, one that neither party will regret. You may get the boss to empathize with you. In the end, however, rather than making a rushed decision within someone else's time frame, it's often better to decline the offer, especially if you feel in your gut that it just isn't right.

How to Ask for a Relocation Package and Moving Expenses

The most common reasons for relocating are starting a new job with a new company, transferring for personal reasons, or being transferred to a new location because of a business need. It's always best to negotiate associated expenses before accepting the job. This way, there are no surprises for you or the company. If negotiating isn't possible, a well-researched plan will contribute to a happy and successful move.

What is the policy on COLAs (cost-of-living adjustments)? It will vary with the company: a salary increase, a down payment for a home, paying points on a mortgage to lower the rate, or providing temporary housing until the employee finds a home are some of the possible options. For more-senior positions, you can negotiate for all of these benefits, not just one of them.

If your schedule permits, make some trips to the new location and explore it. Ask if your employer will consider paying hotel and meal expenses for your family's house-hunting trips.

When in the new city, check out commuter costs and meet with real-estate agents to get some idea of the housing market and property taxes. Get a handle on costs. You want to have enough cash left over after getting your new digs to enjoy and explore your new hometown. So do your research beforehand.

Document your findings, set up a meeting with your new boss, and explain your situation. "If I am to consider the relocation offer you made, we have to discuss the fact that my $250,000 home in Kansas City is comparable to an $800,000 home in San Diego. I will need a cost-of-living adjustment to address that difference. When can we discuss this in detail?"

BE REALISTIC. If your company is very eager to relocate you, a relocation package is negotiable. The more senior you are, the more likely it is that your salary will be based on national, not regional, standards. If you don't have a senior position, and your skills aren't unique, you'll be more limited in what you can ask for. You may have to settle for a bare-bones accommodations. Similarly, if the move is for personal reasons, and not being done at the request or for the benefit of your employer, your position in the negotiation isn't as strong. You'll want to find a way to focus on benefits to the employer in order to bolster your case. For example, while you might be doing the same work, this move will put you in closer proximity to several key clients and allow you to improve customer relations.

DISCUSSING THE MOVE. When discussing moving expenses, make sure to ask that packing expenses and insurance be included. Travel, lodging, fuel, and meals are also things you will want covered during the move. Make sure you understand any exceptions or exclusions in the policy.

Depending on its relocation policy, your company might buy your house if it doesn't sell before you transfer; or the company might reimburse you for the difference between the house's fair market value and what it sells for; or they might pay all the expenses (monthly payments, taxes, and insurance) until your house sells.

Covering real-estate commissions on both the purchase and sale of the house is another benefit you can ask about.

Does your employer have any agreements with national movers? Ask the company to pay the mover directly. Do you have a car or pet that needs to be transported? That's an additional expense, so ask for them to be covered.

MORE THAN MOVING. A relocation package can also include more than just moving expenses. Will your employer assist your spouse in relocating? For example, will it help him with job placement in the new city? Your company may also provide assistance with finding appropriate schools for your children. Advance preparation to help your hubby and little ones feel happy and fulfilled could help ease the transition for all of you and keep the family positioned as your cheering squad.

READ THE FINE PRINT. These moving packages often have a set amount of money allotted to them, and they often hinge on your staying at the company for a minimum amount of time. Find out exactly what the time commitment is and what happens if you leave the company before the end of the relocation term. So that you won't be surprised, ask to see any contract from your employer before you commit to taking the other job and leaving town. Many times employers wait until you arrive at your new destination before handing you a new agreement.

It is very common for companies to demand your repayment of moving expenses if you leave the new job during the first year of employment. Ask about signing bonuses and any other monetary incentives, as you don't want these to be used against you if you end up leaving early while under contract.

NONCOMPETE CLAUSES. These are usually found in employment agreements, so it's a good idea to seek legal advice before you sign a document with such a clause. Some companies utilize these clauses to prevent you from working in your particular industry during a specified amount of time in the event that you leave them.

On the Job

How to Ask for a Raise

It's important to be honest with yourself when wanting a raise. Some people are discouraged with their earnings because they just don't feel appreciated. Others have enhanced their lifestyles—and increased their expenses. Or maybe you're annoyed that your coworker was given a raise and you were not.

Although these are all common motives, they are not the ammunition you need to make your case. Base your request for a raise on accomplishments, not on personal needs. Car payments on your new SUV or your spouse's unemployment are not relevant in the eyes of your employer. You must prove your value—what you're worth—before having any chance at a raise. While many employers are understanding about life issues, sharing your problems will not strengthen your case. That lump in your throat you're feeling about making next month's rent can be your motivation for asking for a raise, but don't kid yourself: your boss is paid to manage the company's bottom line, not your personal finances.

STRIKE WHILE THE IRON'S HOT. Generally, raises are discussed during the annual review process or when the company experiences structural change or substantial increases in profit. Also, if there are changes in the labor market and your skills are in high demand, you may want to ask for a raise. When there's been an increase in your work responsibilities—initiated or adopted—or upon successful completion of an important project that generated great results, or even when you've secured another job offer, that's when it's time to make your move.

MAXIMUM VALUE. There is a difference between the value of *your position* and the value of *you*. A brain surgeon who is employed as a janitor may deserve a brain surgeon's pay, but he will only be paid as a janitor because that is the role he was hired to perform. Similarly, an MBA who's working as a cashier will be compensated as a cashier, not as someone with an advanced degree. Both values play a crucial part in determining salaries, but the position will have a maximum value. Factor this into your plan.

PREP WORK. Because he has his own responsibilities, your employer doesn't know everything you do. Therefore, it's time to pull out the "Look what I've done!" file and brag about yourself—professionally, of course.

What results has your hard work achieved? List any accomplishments of yours that have cut costs, increased revenue or productivity, improved safety or performance, or saved time. Give specific examples, with percentages, facts, and figures, to back up your points. Write a paragraph at the top of this list to summarize your achievements, but think about the bottom-line impact you have made.

In addition to your unique skills, consider the type of business and the area of the country you are in, your education, and your experience. Online salary surveys, career expos, industry organizations, and human-resources professionals can help you to average out national and local salaries.

Know how much you, *in your position*, are worth to your employer. How do your skills and value differ from what others bring to the company? Your argument must support your assertion that you are indeed an asset. Make the case that they can't afford to lose you.

Other factors that will impact discussions on raises include inflation rates; how the company views recruitment, retention, and turnover rates; annual budgets for raises; and how your raise might affect equity within the organization. Check the industry buzz on the company; if there's talk of downsizing, you may want to wait a little while before asking.

RÉSUMÉS AND PAST REVIEWS. Maintain a "me" file that includes notes of praise and appreciation from clients, colleagues and co-workers. Utilize these as tools to show off how far you've advanced and the "good grades" you've earned. The better you perform for the employer, the more money you make for them and the better your chance at a raise.

ANTICIPATE THE OPPOSITION. Figure out in advance why the boss might reject your request for more money. Keep in mind that it's his or her job to keep salaries as tight as possible, which means that saying no isn't usually personal—it's just business. Consider this example: As a magazine editor, perhaps your biggest coup was convincing Angelina Jolie to pose for a cover shoot and grant an exclusive interview. When you tout this accomplishment during the salary review, your boss attempts to diminish your involvement by saying the actress chose the magazine because of its huge circulation, not because of you. Don't back down: stand your ground on your perseverance and negotiating skills while reminding your boss that many other top publications were fighting for the same exclusive—and that you're positive that your role was critical to sealing the deal.

Before the conversation it's key to mentally prepare for the ways the company may try to poke holes in your position. If you've rehearsed the scenarios, you're less likely to be caught off guard, and you'll be more likely to engage in the positive back-and-forth dialogue instead of giving in.

COMMIT. Make an appointment with your boss for a time convenient for both of you. You can send an e-mail or leave a voice mail confidentially requesting to meet in person with him or her to discuss your professional development. If you want to approach the boss directly to request a meeting, good timing is critical. If he or she looks frazzled or is on deadline, now's not a good time to ask.

IN THE ROOM. Bring your list of achievements. Not only will this serve as a guide so that you don't trip yourself up, but it looks professional. Don't sound desperate; sound confident. Do not offer an ultimatum unless you plan to follow through on it.

You may start by saying, "I've been with this company for seven years. While I know that my years of service alone don't merit a raise, I'd like to show you what I've accomplished." Then delve into your points, focusing on quantifiable measures and results.

If you want $4,000 more a year, it's often advisable to ask for $6,000; this will give you a some room to negotiate. You don't want to overwhelm them by asking for $10,000 if your research on comparable salaries tells you that this figure is way out of line, but you also don't want to shortchange yourself. Your boss may say that everyone gets the standard percentage increase. You can respond, "What consideration is made for exceptional employees, up and above the standard cost-of-living increase? How do you reward strong performance? Is it possible for you to revisit this?"

BE REALISTIC. The average raise in this country hovers under 4 percent annually. While you may want significantly more, keep in mind that an employer is balancing what's fair for its whole workforce, not just you.

GET ANOTHER OFFER. Your solid track record of accomplishments may not convince your employer to give you a raise. Your boss may believe that you're paid handsomely to perform effectively. That will change if you announce that you have another job offer, especially if the offer came from a competitor. You do not have to reveal the salary you've been offered; however, you can hint that it's considerably more than what you're getting and that you're prepared to accept it if you can't come to an agreement for a raise. "Since I've been with the company for several years, my preference is to remain in this position. However, I would require a substantial increase in base pay, especially since the other company is offering much more than I currently earn. Are you willing to discuss such an increase?"

OUT THE DOOR? As a final bargaining chip, you can indicate that you'll have to resign if your salary requests aren't met. This is not advisable unless you are truly prepared to leave. For some people, it's difficult to maintain their morale and performance when they feel underpaid. They'd rather be unemployed than tolerate their current salary level. Unless you can afford to be unemployed and without any income, and you're ready to explain to another prospective employer why you're out of work, do not contemplate this option. You may gently remind your boss that it's often difficult and costly for an employer to recruit, train, and invest in a new person. This could open up a second chance for discussion.

NO RAISE, OTHER OPTIONS. If you feel you've gone above and beyond the call of duty in your position, you may want to ask for a promotion: a new position and a new title, with the potential of a higher salary now or at some point down the road. You'd argue for more money because you're taking on additional responsibilities. If more money is not possible, ask for more vacation days, flexible hours, or a bigger bonus at year-end if these are of interest to you.

If your boss feels you don't merit a raise at this time, then ask what you can do to improve your job skills or performance, and what results you need to show in order to receive a raise or bonus. Ask for a timetable and schedule a meeting at which he or she can reevaluate your performance and pay.

How to Ask for a Buyout

Every day, companies experience financial difficulty. Companies that have announced takeovers or layoffs or have to reduce head count may want to release you, and to do so a way that is mutually agreeable. Much of the time they will require you to waive your rights to legal action in exchange for a severance or buyout.

AN END AND A BEGINNING. If you've been at the company for a few years but aren't too disappointed at the news, you can suggest a mutual-consent resignation. If your position is eliminated and you've been at the company for only a short time, you may have no

She Asked for It!

The most challenging thing I ever did was to ask for a raise. At a previous job, I was in management and was receiving a typical cost-of-living pay increase once a year. I knew that I wanted, needed, and deserved more, but I also knew that my boss was not the type to accept "Please give me a better raise because I've earned it!" So, I presented him with a few creative options on paper, showing what I contributed to the bottom line and how any of my options for a pay increase would provide incentive to me without affecting his bottom line. The results, after some back and forth, were favorable, and I was successful in increasing my salary by a significant amount.

—NANCY KRAMER JOFFRE, *account executive, WSTR-FM Atlanta*

choice but to quit or be laid off. If you're ready to retire, here's your chance. If you are looking to change your career or start your own company, this is your big break.

However, a buyout package is not all sparkle and shimmer. Be careful. There are many crucial points to consider, some of which are listed below. You'll be relinquishing regular salary and benefits, and the payout is often contingent on specific terms. If you don't comply with them, you could be required to pay back a lot of money. You need a smart plan of attack in order to make your exit as beneficial as possible.

She Asked for It!

The first time I had to renegotiate a contract was terribly intimidating. I wanted to stay at my station, but I didn't need to stay. That meant I wanted the station to make significant changes to prove they considered me a valuable asset. While I knew I deserved these things, I'm a southern girl—polite and sometimes hesitant in this kind of situation. But I realized, too, that the men in the newsroom never had any trouble asking for what they wanted.

I wrote out a list that covered not only the things I wanted, but also the reasons I deserved them. The list included what I felt I had contributed to the team, examples of times I went above and beyond the original job expectations, and detailed research about how people in similar positions were being compensated.

I practiced how I would say everything. I played out the conversation in my head over and over until I knew exactly how I wanted it to come out. I didn't sleep much the few days before the meeting, but I knew my stuff cold.

I'd be lying if I said my voice wasn't quavering a little as I started discussing things with my boss, but my nervousness didn't last long. I knew my points were solid, and it felt good to say all those things out loud. I left the table with exactly what I wanted, which was wonderful. But the real reward was the feeling that came with standing up for myself. I definitely stood a few inches taller after that—and not because of my three-inch heels!

—JENNIFER GLADSTONE, *news anchor, News Central/*
Sinclair Broadcast Group

IMPORTANT POINTS AND SUCCESSFUL STRATEGIES INCLUDE:

- If you want to shoot for the early-retirement package, here are a few things for you to know. TOWBPA (the Older Workers' Benefit Protection Act) stipulates that companies must offer employees ages 40 and older at least 21 days to consider a buyout offer. If you accept the package, ask them to recalculate your pension as if you're already at retirement age, so that your benefits aren't drastically reduced.

- Since lump-sum payments might be part of the buyout, remember that you will be required to pay taxes, so your net amount won't look so appealing. The buyout could also push you into a higher tax bracket. Therefore, ask if you can spread your buyout over several months to avoid the jump in income. Speak with a tax consultant and a lawyer prior to signing any agreement. Discuss your options with them. You don't want the buyout money to work against you.

- The proper time at which to approach the powers that be will depend on what kind of situation the company is facing and how extreme the atmosphere is. Use common sense and your own judgment in the workplace. It might be best to casually approach the supervisor and ask who is the proper person to meet with. Then schedule the meeting, giving yourself at least a day to get your thoughts aligned. Asking for a meeting now will allow you more time to think about the situation before everyone else gets frenzied. "I realize we were just informed of the takeover and the proceedings will be happening in the next few months, but could I meet with you tomorrow? As the senior marketing manager I'd like to understand my options, especially if my peers or direct reports start coming to me for advice or information."

- Feel free to ask for more severance pay than the often-standard 1 or 2 weeks per year served. Those in more-senior positions might be able to negotiate in the range of 6-to-18 months.

- Don't overlook health benefits. Under certain circumstances, such as voluntary or involuntary job loss, employees and their families have the right under the Consolidated Omnibus Budget Reconciliation Act (COBRA) to continue, for limited periods of time, the group health benefits provided by their group health plan. Qualified individuals may be required to pay up to 102 percent of the cost of the plan. Since this can be very expensive, ask your employer to consider extending their portion of your benefit for the length of the severance period.

- Bargain for other benefits. You can ask for outplacement services, which may assist you in landing a new position; payout for remaining sick days or vacation days; and even living expenses if you were recently relocated.

- Put your questions in writing and request written responses from the company. Save hard copies of these and all related paperwork and e-mails.

- Ask to be notified of any improved buyout packages in the interim. These are unlikely given the legal challenges. However, unless you ask, the employer isn't required to inform you of better deals. If you don't ask, you'll be stuck with a lesser package.

- If you want to look for another job in your field, make sure there isn't a noncompete clause in your buyout contract. If there is and you cannot negotiate it, you will need to talk to a legal adviser or think about a different field.

- Be aware of any loans you may owe, such as borrowings against your 401k, since these will come due when you leave. You can ask for these loans to be paid off as part of the buyout.

- Be conscious of deadlines, especially since they're usually firm. However, if you're confused or uncomfortable about any aspect of a potential buyout, don't rush to sign anything that may waive your rights or commit you to terms with which you're unfamiliar. Instead, seek professional legal and tax advice.

Overall, remember to negotiate with humility. Be ready for your requests to be rejected and for a lively give-and-take to ensue. Remove your emotions and don't take things personally. Start conversations with a clear head and a smart focus on what you want, which is the best package possible.

How to Ask Your Employer to Support a Charitable Cause

Most employers commit themselves to philanthropic causes in order to show that they care about the community and to demonstrate leadership. When an employee is willing to take the steps necessary to approach her employer about a cause she is passionate about, or about an opportunity to do good, the manager or leader is often ap-

She Asked for It!

I think the most challenging thing I've ever asked for in my career was to be released from a brand-new four-year contract. It was a wonderful company, one of the biggest and best in the television world. The president of the company had promoted me, moved me across the country, and invested in me. But within a few months of the move, I realized it wasn't the right situation for me. There was nothing wrong, and the project was going well. I just knew in my gut this wasn't a match.

This was extremely daunting to me because, maybe like a lot of women, I didn't like to cause problems. Not to mention, I was contractually obligated to do the job I signed on for. The company was known for holding people to their contracts; after all, contracts are supposed to be binding. The company had every right to tell

(continued)

preciative, provided the discussion does not impact work performance. There are effective ways to ask your employer for financial support for a worthwhile cause. But first, go ahead and give yourself a pat on the back for thinking of others.

BEFORE THE MEETING.

- Do your homework. Asking your employer to get involved in a charitable cause requires knowledge, research, and personal passion. Before asking your employer to support a cause, consider doing it the same way you might ask any potential donor me to get over myself and do the job I had agreed to do. I didn't have another job lined up; I knew I wasn't in a legal or ethical position to pursue another job somewhere else.

I went to the president of the company before I spoke a single word to anyone else about my problem. When I spoke to him, for once I didn't try to explain everything that was on my mind or to justify myself. I didn't fall all over myself apologizing. I didn't blame anybody or bad-mouth anybody. I just said, "I'm not happy. This is a great job, you have been wonderful to me, but I need to make a change."

He generously accepted my need to go. We had a painless negotiation and then terminated the contract. We parted a few months later on very good terms.

—TRACY GREEN, *executive vice president, Lion Television USA*

for money. Begin by determining what causes your employer is interested in and what is important to the senior management. Understand the priorities of the organization and of your boss, since he or she will ultimately be the internal champion of your cause. Make a list of the questions you will ask and the statements you will make. For example, "Mr. O'Connor, I know you sit on the board of a literacy, group so I know how important educational issues are to you. I want to talk to you about another cause I believe you will find equally worthwhile."

• Next, research the cause and organization you are pitching. Have you been personally involved with it? Can you answer questions about how this organization will benefit from the donation of time, money, or other resources that your company might make? Do you know what the organization stands for? How do they spend their money? Is the organization a government-recognized charity, so that donations are tax-deductible? Know as much as you can so that you can show your level of commitment. To demonstrate your passion, share a personal story; for example, "When I volunteered last weekend at the adult learning center, I encountered so many wonderful, deserving people who are eager to build their skills." There's nothing more effective than a personal story for giving your message the ring of authenticity.

- Build a business case. Sometimes your interest is personal, other times it's professional. Your research has determined that it would be smart business to support a charity. "Since we want to reach more women as potential customers, I suggest we sponsor a team for the breast cancer walk."

- Armed with information, determine who's the decision maker or opinion leader you should meet with. If you work for a large organization, ask your boss to steer you to the right person and support your efforts. If your company has an internal foundation, who can advise you about it ahead of time? Is there a protocol to follow with these types of requests? Search for a fellow employee who has presented a cause to the proper decision maker and ask for insights and tips on successful strategies.

DURING THE MEETING.

- Keep in mind that you are talking to busy people who have limited time. Consider the questions that will be asked of you as well as those that you will be asking. One of the most powerful things you can convey is how the company would benefit from being involved with this charity. Employers like to support groups that their employees are interested and involved in. As a company initiative, some will even match what employees give. Companies want to have people who feel good about the company they work for, and often a charitable connection goes a long way toward achieving this. Be prepared to address this point. Show how people are already involved and interested in your cause, even in the absence of a formal program or affiliation. For example, "In the last six months, more than 100 of our employees have donated money to the Red Cross. I know there's a strong desire to contribute time as well."

- Next, identify the individuals who are going to be impacted. If you've been helped by the services of this organization, make that connection known. Think visually so that you can show who will benefit from your company's good deeds and actions. Share a few photographs or a brochure about the organization. Bring along something to leave behind about the organization, including its annual report and information kit if available.

- Make it as easy as possible for your employer to say yes. If you make it simple for your employer to follow through with your request, then you dramatically increase your chance of success. "I want our company to be a sponsor of this fun run. Here are the sponsorship papers that detail all of the costs and benefits. You can already see that other prominent groups are committed to participating, and here's a list of those who've pledged their financial support." Also, strengthen your request by showing what other companies and even the competition are doing. Then be clear about what you're asking: Do you want your company to be a title sponsor? Do you want management to sponsor a company team? Do you want permission to solicit the participation of other employees?

- Be very specific. After asking for a donation, avoid saying things like, "Anything you can do is fine." Don't apologize for asking for money with statements such as, "I know that times are tight and that I should have come to you a few months ago." Instead, you will want to say, "This is a deserving organization and a very worthwhile project. Our company would benefit greatly by getting involved. I'd like you to consider a $5,000 donation." And then be quiet, even if it means sitting in silence as you await a response. If the decision maker asks for more time, try to nail a follow-up meeting: "When would you suggest that I check back in with you so that we don't miss out on all of the benefits of this affiliation? I want to make sure we get full credit and exposure for our involvement before it's too late."

AFTER THE MEETING.

- Immediately, write a thank-you note. Thank your employer for the meeting and recap what you requested. If a commit-

She Asked for It!

Because of what I do, I'm always in the position of having to ask for donors. I know we're doing important work to help children, but the fear of being turned down is very real. You can't take it personally. What I have learned is that I may not always be the best person for the task. So I learned to ask for assistance: I involved the community, which helped to do the asking. It's okay to depend on others if there's a common goal. The unexpected prize for me was that I became a leader in fund-raising, and the children have benefited because of the community support.

—SUSAN TAUBER, *founder and executive director,*
the Adaptive Learning Center

ment has not yet been given, or if your request was denied, continue to express your appreciation for management's consideration and politely suggest that they reconsider your suggestion in the months ahead or in the next fiscal year.

- If the company does contribute a gift, thank the decision maker immediately. If it's tied to a specific event, such as a marathon or fund-raiser, be sure to follow up with a complete report on how your company was represented. This may include copies of brochures featuring the company logo, a list of employees who participated, photographs of the event, media coverage that was generated, and any other relevant materials. "I want to thank you again for the generous donation and want you to know what our company's involvement accomplished.

Over $500,000 was raised, and I was so proud of our company, which was one of the top donors. We had 300 employees participate, and the experience was very rewarding for each of them. If it's acceptable to you, I'd like to keep you updated a few times a year about the continued success of this effort."

Stay dedicated to the cause and consider your important role as you build a bridge between your workplace and a nonprofit cause you are passionate about.

Contributor: David Williams, president and chief executive officer of Make-A-Wish Foundation of America

How to Ask for an Expense Account

Be confident when asking for additional perks for your position, especially if they will benefit the company in some way. An expense account can fit this criterion.

If you didn't negotiate an expense account before accepting the job offer or you aren't clear about what expenses the company might be willing to cover, you can certainly look into these matters at any point during your employment. You should start by composing a detailed summary of what you do, what you'd like to do, and how these would benefit the company.

WHO NEEDS ONE? Does your job entail entertaining current or prospective clients, or is this an idea you'd like to implement now? How will entertaining clients help you meet your goals and also help the company?

Depending on your position and seniority, list all possible expenses that you would likely anticipate: meals, car rentals, fuel reimbursements, parking, airline or train tickets, lodging, birthday gifts, sporting events, etc. Make sure you understand the ethics involved with incurring such expenses, especially if you will be entertaining current or prospective clients and/or giving gifts to those same people. Many companies have strict guidelines as to the value of the gifts its employees may receive. In some cases, there is a prohibition on gifts, including expensive meals and tickets to theater or sporting events. So think twice before asking for an expense account to cover this type of spending.

If you're traveling more for work, you're no doubt incurring a range of expenses. If the topic of reimbursement hasn't been fully explored, this is probably a good time to address it.

Are you climbing up the corporate ladder and attending more seminars, industry functions, and business-related parties? Show how receiving more training and attending these events will help you to achieve better results for the company. You may also want to offer to share any new information with your colleagues through e-mail or "lunch-and-learn" sessions. This will spread out the cost to the employer since more people will benefit from the knowledge and information. In addition, you'll have a unique opportunity to showcase your leadership and presentation skills.

If you're working for a small business, do you run errands for the company that involve outlays for fuel, postal and delivery services, and office supplies? Such costs may justify some type of expense accounting.

DETAIL YOUR REPORT. Once you've outlined what expenses are most likely and appropriate for your position, consider what the company can realistically afford. If you're working for a small start-up, there's a good chance that wining and dining prospective clients at the most expensive restaurant in town won't go over well with management. If you're employed by a Fortune 500 company and you're expected to entertain top clients, then such an expense would likely be reasonable and justified.

Are you a resourceful employee who looks for good values and would spend money wisely? Don't hesitate to mention this if you're a conservative and conscientious spender.

Before approaching your boss, pinpoint a monthly figure that you'd anticipate spending, along with how it will be spent. For example, one client lunch per week, at an average of $75 per meal, would mean about $300 a month. Taxis, parking, and fuel would be additional related expenses. If acknowledging key clients or vendors with birthday gifts is important to your line of work, determine an approximate budget and frequency as part of your proposal.

When you're ready to present your request to your boss, be clear about the business impact. "Because I'm now traveling for my position, there are a number of expenses I'm incurring, and I'd like to discuss an expense account." Or perhaps you'd say, "Since I'm taking on additional sales and client relations, I'll be entertaining customers on a regular basis. For this reason, we should discuss an expense account for this business spending."

Ask if you'll receive a corporate credit card or a cash advance, or if you'll be expected to front the money and submit receipts for reimbursement. If your personal finances make it difficult to lay out the money on behalf of your employer, ask your boss to authorize a cash advance, for which you would submit timely receipts that support agreed-upon expenses. Keep in mind that you'll have to justify all expenses even if incurred with a company-issued credit card.

If there's any hesitation on the part of your boss about agreeing to company-reimbursed expenses, offer to start with a three-month trial period. During that time you should stick to the types of expenses, as well as the dollar limits, that you agreed to in advance. If you venture outside of the terms you initially discussed, you risk having the expenses rejected, which means you'll be out of the money you spent.

Be prepared to show on a quarterly basis how the company is benefiting from your spending. To keep track of your expenses, start a spreadsheet from Day One, and use it to record all expenses incurred and the result(s) of each expenditure.

How to Ask for a Company Car and Travel Expenses

Benefits such as a company car are typically viewed as necessary for sales professionals or traveling service personnel. They also provide incentives for up-and-coming employees and rewards for senior management.

If you don't fit into any of the categories in which a company car is customary, you will need to present strong reasons why you should be driving one. You will be coming up against the nature and level of your job, as well as the company's policies and protocol on such benefits. Since this is a much more complicated and difficult argument than, say, asking for a few extra days off, you must decide if you have enough substantive ammunition to justify asking for a car.

IMMEDIATE CONCERNS. Given that this isn't one of those no-brainer requests that any employer would approve easily, you'll have to engage in some serious planning:

How would the company benefit from giving you a car? Perhaps you'll leave the company if your request isn't met, and your departure would be a significant loss to the employer. From the management's perspective, would it be more beneficial to give you the car than to replace you? Is a car necessary for you to perform your duties? If you're in pharmaceutical sales, your employer knows that you have to carry around samples to multiple appointments daily, which means a car is essential. Since the drug company doesn't want its employees showing up in clunkers, it behooves them to provide suitable cars for all sales reps. An automobile is a reflection on your employer and you, and a company-paid car ensures a certain standard. Why is a company car essential for your duties? Explain why you shouldn't have to use your own vehicle for these purposes. Ordinarily, the mere need to travel to and from work doesn't justify a request for a company car. You'll need to address why you deserve such a benefit. Will giving you a company car be unfair to your peers or viewed as preferential treatment? Who will cover all of the related costs, such as insurance, taxes, parking, fuel, tolls, and maintenance and repairs?

Research company protocol to determine when and if company cars are provided. To whom have they been awarded and under what circumstances? If no precedent exists, you'll have to plead extraordinary circumstances. Among the possibilities:

- You're the only person in the company who's required to drive 200 miles a week to visit the production facility. While those random checks are essential to quality assurance, they're taking a toll on your vehicle.

- You have a very long commute, which resulted from your office relocating or a change in territories. It's putting excessive mileage on your car, which is eight years old.

- Your promotion requires you to visit high-profile clients and often drive them around for site visits. Your own two-door car isn't suitable for such use.

- Your company has been renting a car regularly for you to use while making sales calls, and it would be more cost-effective to lease or buy one for your exclusive use.

START YOUR ENGINE. You'll want to use precedent, along with your well-thought-out responses to the questions posed above, when making your pitch to the boss. Keep in mind that there are many different situations that require a company car, but the whole matter hinges on your showing your employer that you are a desirable resource. Your responsibilities, not to mention the extra work you've been accomplishing, create the need for company transportation; your job should not entail putting extra wear and tear on your personal vehicle. You must prove—through sales, profits, increased client contact, and more—that the company is benefiting from your service and efficiency. Your employer must see—through your pitch—that it is to its advantage to provide you with this significant perk.

If you're rejected, don't walk away empty-handed. Focus on other benefits tied to transportation. The company won't pay for a car, but perhaps they'll cover parking, a portion of your insurance, a per diem based on mileage for work-related driving, a monthly gas allotment, or a bonus toward the purchase of a new vehicle for you. Any or all of these options would be justified if you're using your own vehicle for important and essential company business on a regular basis.

How to Ask for a Loan

There are different reasons why people approach their companies for loans. They may be struggling financially and need immediate assistance. They may have a son or daughter ready for college and need to fund their education. There may be unexpected or nonreimbursed medical expenses. They may need a down payment for a home, or want to avoid losing their existing home.

DO I DARE ASK? Although loans are usually reserved for executive management, you may still be able to negotiate one if you're able to prove yourself an asset to the company. Company policy and the reason for the loan are big factors in how you should present your request to your superiors. Depending on your relationship with management and how openly you can speak, you will emphasize either the actual nature of the loan request or how it will improve your performance.

One example: "I've been with the company for five years, and you know I wouldn't ask for this unless I could back it up. I need to talk about some kind of loan from the company. You know I have a proven track record of bringing in clients and topping the sales charts. Right now I need to take care of my husband's medical bills, which are burdening us. Can we discuss some terms and conditions that you might find acceptable?"

Since employers aren't in the business of making loans to standard-position employees, no matter how great their performance, you'll need to have great information to back up your reasons for asking. Similarly, a small-business owner might not have the available cash to make such a loan or might not be willing or able to take such a risk. Your request might be viewed in a negative way, so it's important to carefully think this through. Depending on the nature of your employment, there are some options you may want to consider first. Each option requires you to approach a different person in the organization, so as you consider your next steps, keep in mind where you have the strongest relationships.

- If you work for a small employer, ask the top boss for an advance on a bonus that you'll be eligible for down the road. In addition, you could agree to forgo vacation days in lieu of extra pay, or you could share your willingness to take on extra work after hours.

- Consider borrowing against your 401k. There are strict guidelines to follow, so do your homework before taking money out of your future to finance your present. 401k loans are legal, but employers aren't required to participate. Small businesses typically can't afford the high administrative costs these plans incur. Your employer can also specify the allowable reasons for a loan, such as education expenses or the first-time purchase of a home. You may be able to borrow from the account as long as a required minimum amount remains. Sometimes your plan will require spousal consent before you can access the loan. Repayment of the loan is often deducted from your paycheck, so you can consult your human-resources department about the specific procedures. If you leave your job, the balance of the loan will be due in full, usually within a brief period.

- Ask your direct supervisor about an advance on commission. You may feel more justified in receiving this kind of funding, and the desire to earn it back will spur you to do more for the company.

- See a credit union for a loan. Credit-union loans typically have better rates than other loans and are easy to access for employees in good standing.

- Ask your human-resources department about the availability of employee-assistance loans. Many companies offer these to help their employees through challenging times, thus providing them with much-needed acknowledgment, boosting their morale, and securing their loyalty. These kinds of assistance loans also require agreements to be signed and involve certain stipulations, which vary by employer. Commonly, you must be a full-time employee and on payroll, with at least six months of service; only one loan can be taken per year; there is a maximum loan amount unless a greater amount is approved by a superior; there are loan fees, and the loan will need to be paid back by a certain time and will be deducted from payroll checks.

TAKE YOUR PICK. You want to find a loan that suits your need and that you can repay without being a servant to the loan for years to come. If after researching all of the available options, you determine that asking your employer for a loan is the best route for you, plan in advance by anticipating the possible objections. Don't assume that your company has the funds available. Figure out ahead of time the reasons why your boss might say no, and then come up with responses. For example, the boss says the company has never granted such loans and doesn't want to start now. If you're a very valuable employee who produces exceptional results, you can say that, without the loan, you'll be required to take an evening or week-end job to supplement your income. Even though you must be clear that this won't negatively impact your commitment to your main job, which of course is your priority, your boss might realize that it's not in his or her best interest for you to work around the clock. The company might be willing to negotiate terms to assist you if doing so means preventing you from taking on a part-time job.

Your employer may refer you to an alternate assistance program or consumer-credit counseling, depending on your particular hardship. Be open to their advice since asking for a loan isn't the same as asking for an extended deadline or discussing sick days. This is a much bigger issue and needs to be handled appropriately.

Depending on the nature of your loan request and who you are—a senior employee, or a newer one with fewer options—be sure to thank your boss for his time. Under no circumstances should you state or imply that the company's failure to honor your request will result in a decline in your performance or that it will negatively impact your commitment to your position. Tell your boss how much you appreciate his consideration and confidentiality and assure him that resolving this situation can only affect you and your performance positively.

How to Ask for a New Computer or Expensive Office Equipment

A technical giant like IBM or Dell will likely have the most innovative equipment on the market; and if you work for them, you won't need to go begging for replacements.

But what about the small and medium-sized companies that do

not replace computers as often, or don't invest in the newest technology? These companies tend to have fewer employees and smaller budgets. Computers crash, copiers fizzle, and scanners just buzz.

WRITTEN PROPOSAL. It's often cheaper and wiser to invest in new technology than to waste time and money trying to save a dud, but that's not always apparent to the person writing the checks. The best way to ask for a new computer or other expensive equipment is to create a thoughtful bottom-line-focused proposal and present it in person. If you can have some coworkers join you for the meeting—those that use the same equipment—your request will be taken more seriously and considered less frivolous by your employer.

Your position must be that the new technology will increase efficiency, save money, or generate new business by improving processes. Do your research and get a handful of different quotes from various sellers so that you can compare costs. Find out what payment options are available, and whether the equipment would be purchased or leased.

Have two prongs to the proposal: one for all the equipment on your wish list, and the other for the bare minimum. No matter how successful your presentation, your company's budget and the opinion of your boss will decide which proposal is chosen. To make the choice as easy as possible for your employer, have the prices listed and your selections ready.

DETAIL YOUR DILEMMAS. It's not enough to simply announce that you want something new. You must explain succinctly how or why the purchase would benefit your performance and the company's bottom line.

- If you're working on an old computer that breaks down often, you're losing time you need to carry out your work and produce results. Make clear that the company has spent hundreds of dollars on technical support in the last three months for this machine alone, which isn't prudent. Buying a new computer would mean avoiding such wasteful costs such costs and would enable you to do your job much faster. Fewer delays, fewer frustrations, and increased productivity, all of which are beneficial to the company.

- You've spent $500 in the last three months making color copies at Kinko's. For client presentations it is necessary to have crisp and perfect color copies, which aren't possible on your black-and-white office machine. Buying a color copier would save time and money.

- Now that you're on the road a lot for your position, it would make sense to have a company-paid Blackberry and cell phone, which require onetime costs to purchase the devices, plus monthly service fees. Using these devices will mean better customer service and quicker communication between colleagues.

Help your boss to see that expensive office equipment can improve a company's professional image, boost employee morale, and ultimately increase productivity. It can even make work more enjoyable, because employees will know they are gaining experience on updated devices and getting the job done more quickly. In the case of truly sophisticated machinery, offer your boss a training session so that he can experience the new equipment for himself.

Be respectful of budget constraints. If the money just isn't there or they just won't budge, ask if the company would consider leasing equipment, with the option to buy down the road.

LEASING OFFICE EQUIPMENT. Leasing is an option if money is tight. It can improve cash flow since it frees up funds for the company to use toward other necessary expenses. Leasing is typically easier to arrange than financing, which may require a strong credit history. And it offers the advantage of helping your company to keep up with technology, which is especially important if the company needs to stay on the cutting edge. Signing up for a series of short-term leases may be less expensive than buying new equipment. There are even update packages for lease plans, which will enable your company to modernize automatically and save money at the same time.

If you're rejected outright, ask when it would be appropriate to follow up and try again. In the meantime, continue to document money spent that could have been saved if new equipment were available. Track time lost or wasted as well, since these data will give you strong evidence when you revisit the issue.

How to Ask for Company-Sponsored Child Care

From on-site centers to off-site backup options subsidized by employers, child care has become an enormously important issue in the workplace. After all, it's a significant expense that working parents incur in order to care for their adorable little creatures. If your employer doesn't have any such provisions in its benefits package, you may be able to initiate such services through careful research and a smart presentation that focuses on the financial benefits to the employer.

She Asked for It!

Believe it or not, the most challenging thing I asked for was a cell phone. Many years ago, before every walking creature had a cell phone, I was offered what I thought at the time was an amazing job on the morning show of the top radio station in the market. Problem was, the radio station was in the next state over, and so the job meant a two-hour drive every morning, beginning at 2:30 A.M.

Salary and benefits were all worked out. Then I asked for the unthinkable—a cell phone, which would let me be in touch with the producer of the show and make the two-hour ride productive.

As smoothly as the contract negotiations had gone, they would not budge on providing me with a cell phone. As difficult a decision as it was, I ended up turning the job down.

It was no longer about the cell phone; rather, the wrangling over such a small issue told me this company didn't get the big picture. I was heartbroken over losing the opportunity. Two years later I was offered a bigger job in a bigger market on a bigger show.

—SUE COPE, *Boston news reporter and morning-show personality*

There are three main types of benefits: back-up care, subsidized daycare, and on-site child care. Backup care is usually needed whenever your regular child-care arrangements are not available. This may be when either your child or your provider is sick, when your provider is on vacation or quits unexpectedly, or when schools are closed. Many employers recognize that by assisting employees when child-care arrangements break down or children are sick, they reduce unscheduled absences and save themselves money. Some employers subsidize a portion of the cost of backup care for their employees. Other companies sponsor arrangements by setting aside backup-care availability at a local service, developing a program at the work site, or providing service in an employee's home.

Subsidized daycare means the employer is paying a portion of the costs. Some companies negotiate favorable discounted rates for employees. Of course on-site child care is many parents' dream, but the high costs associated with this benefit prevent it from being a common reality.

RESEARCH THE NEED. If your company does not provide any form of child-care benefits, you should research the need for them among employees. If your colleagues are mostly childless, the company is not likely to jump at your request, since the perks would only benefit a minority of the workforce. In such a case, depending on your position, you might be able to negotiate additional compensation to contribute to your child-care costs much the same way you'd negotiate for any other benefit. The employer must see an advantage in approving your request; in some cases this advantage might simply be retaining you as an employee. If, on the flip side, your research reveals that a majority of employees might benefit from or be interested in child-care programs, then you have a foundation on which to build a broader case.

Research companies in your industry and your area that provide child-care benefits to their employees. You can do this by talking to people with children about their solutions, searching online, referencing popular lists that rank best employers in the country, and visiting child-care centers to inquire about affiliations with local employers. Ask about rates for employers. (These rates tend to be based on the number of eligible employees.)

GATHER THE FACTS. Child-care issues are the leading cause of family-related problems in the workplace, including tardiness and absenteeism. In the United States child-care-related absenteeism costs businesses more than $3 billion annually, which means that employers have the opportunity to significantly increase morale and dramatically decrease absenteeism by initiating child-care programs. Similarly, the availability of such a benefit can be used to attract and retain some of the best talent in your industry and geographic area.

If hard data about missed work at your company aren't readily available to you, try to gather anecdotal information from colleagues with kids. Any employer would want to know how its own troops are affected by personal challenges.

MAKE A PITCH. Unless your direct boss is part of senior management, she is not likely to have much decision-making authority on this issue. You'll want to ask her to tell you whom she thinks you should approach with your request, and to help you set up such a meeting. "Child-care is an important issue to many of my colleagues here. I'd appreciate your assistance in helping to arrange a meeting for me with the head of human resources so that I can present research on the possibility of child-care assistance benefits. I strongly believe the company should consider such a program as a cost-saving initiative."

You don't want to start off by making demands. Instead, you want to open up a dialogue. Focus the conversation on the needs of both the organization and its employees, including you. You want to make clear that child-care issues impact employees, their families, and the employer, especially since in today's highly competitive workplace there are many more issues governing employment decisions and even employee performance than the usual salary, bonuses, and vacation time.

Be prepared to be specific. Depending on your circumstances, you might say, "I wanted to let you know that I'm pregnant. I'm very excited about starting a family, and I'm equally committed to my professional career. As you no doubt know, one of the challenges that face families is child care. As I explore various options, I realize that company-supported programs are a win-win for both the employees and employers."

If you're working for a small company, or one without the need for a significant commitment to this benefit, ask for a shared expense. For example, "From a financial standpoint, reliable child care will cost me $10,000 a year. I'm hoping you'll consider subsidizing a portion of that cost. Knowing that my child is in good hands will give me peace of mind and allowing to continue traveling for work with the usual stability. Considering my compensation and position in the company, the cost of a subsidy seems insignificant compared to the great reward the company will receive."

If you work for a large company where many people would benefit from such a program, you'll want to request that a more significant program be put into place. Don't expect overnight solutions or a quick commitment. Schedule follow-up meetings and continue to gather facts and anecdotes to support your case.

Professional
Advancement

Onward and Upward

How to Ask for Face-Time with the Boss

You have something very important or even critical to tell or ask your boss. Depending on the company and its policies and dynamics, you might not be able to walk right in and speak up. You also might be fearful of taking the plunge and sharing whatever is on your mind. Regardless of your situation, asking for face-time with the head person can be daunting, but that doesn't mean you have to take a backseat to your fears and deny yourself the right to speak up. Sure, there's always a risk of being thought of as a kiss-up, but your chumminess with the bigwig just might prove to be one of your smartest career accelerators. Here are some valuable strategies for making it happen.

SEEK ASSISTANCE. If you must go through an assistant, be prepared to reveal the topic of discussion, the nature of your desired meeting, and the expected time you'll require of your boss. Since it is the assistant's job to manage the boss's schedule and to minimize or limit unnecessary meetings, don't be insulted if she says no or grills you on why you really need the face time. Be ready for her to suggest that you meet with someone else instead. Tell her why you must meet with the boss. You'll have a much-greater chance of success if you ask for 10 to 15 minutes versus 30 minutes or more. If you're well prepared, you won't need a lot of time to make your point. If he winds up wanting to talk longer because he's interested in hearing more, so be it.

If the boss doesn't have an assistant, you can either e-mail or call him to schedule a time to meet. Be clear about your intentions. "I'd like to schedule 15 minutes this week to review the Phillips project. What time would be best for you?" When asking in person, always be ready for the boss to say he's willing to discuss it that moment. If your request pertains to you and your performance, say so up front. It's never wise to ambush someone. "I'd like to schedule 15 minutes this week to discuss my performance. I have some ideas that I'd like your feedback on. What time would be best for you?"

PENCIL IT IN. There are several reasons why the boss might agree to hear what you have to say:

- You have a great idea on how to save money or make money.

- You've proven yourself to be an asset to the company, and now you want to discuss your potential there.

- You have to bring a confidential problem to his attention.

- You have to notify him discreetly of something he's been doing wrong.

OVERPREPARE. Do yourself a favor and overprepare for this meeting. You do not want to waste your boss's time since this would likely reflect poorly on you. To avoid fumbling through your notes and forgetting exactly what you want to say, create an outline with bulleted statements consisting of the main points that you want to discuss. These points should include not only the outline of where you want to lead the meeting, but the essential elements that must be stressed. Those tend to be the key points that determine the success of the entire meeting. If you assign a beginning point, a middle point, and an ending point to each topic in advance of the meeting, you will be able to fill in the ideas once you start talking.

Keep your thoughts concise. To keep yourself from rambling on and on the way many of us do when we get nervous, rehearse what you want to say. Don't make statements that you can't back up. You may be embarrassed if you're asked to elaborate on what you just said.

For example, you can't walk into his office with a file and a smile and say, "I can make us one million dollars a year—trust me" without presenting specifics, charts, or spreadsheets on how you plan to do it. You also can't have a meeting in order to accuse a coworker of a slipup in ethics unless you have proof that extends beyond hearsay. "Well, I overheard a conversation in the lunchroom about Jack sending inappropriate e-mails, and we've got to do something about it." If you're going to make such a claim, be ready to back it up.

SEEK A SOLUTION. If the purpose of your meeting is to present a problem, be sure you're prepared to follow up with a recommended solution, a range of scenarios, or some suggested methods of working toward a resolution. Don't just add to the headache—cure it. Otherwise, you may be labeled a complainer. For example, "I've discovered that there's a serious flaw in the production cycle. I have a technical expert ready to help troubleshoot the problem if you're willing to approve this expense." Another option: "We're over budget on the project, so I've identified three specific areas where we'll be able to save money to compensate."

Once you've presented all the facts and possible solutions, give your boss the helm. Listen. Let him take charge. Heed his advice. Thank him and get his answers or approvals in writing, if applicable. You can do this discreetly by saying, "Thank you, Bill, for your time. I know this is a busy week for you, yet this discussion was high-priority for my team and me. I will type up some notes to summarize today's meeting and drop them by for your approval. Would that be okay?" Follow up if you don't hear back in a timely manner about the steps to take after the meeting.

How to Ask for a New Title

Twenty years ago, the rungs up the corporate ladder were laid out: stay with one company for ten years, and you'd become a vice president. Today, people change jobs much more frequently, and titles are often ambiguous. However, each new position you take ideally should include a promotion in job title. Yet title remains an often-overlooked method of building your career. Not only can a significant title open doors on the job, it helps professionals climb the corporate ladder—especially when switching companies.

If you enjoy your position but are displeased with your title, there are several smart ways to approach your boss about making a change. But first, be honest with yourself: why do you really want a new title? It could be that your peers who perform the same functions enjoy titles more prestigious than yours. Perhaps you want the perceived

She Asked for It!

I invented a product called Spanx that makes women look a size smaller and that erases panty lines. I was sitting in my apartment, and I called up Neiman Marcus and asked for the hosiery buyer. I didn't know it at the time, but what I did was very unusual, since everyone else sets up a booth at trade shows, hoping to be discovered by a buyer. I trusted my gut, picked up the phone, called, and asked. I said, "I'm Sara Blakely, and I invented a product that will change women's lives. If you'll give me ten minutes of your time, I'll fly to Dallas and show you how."

The buyer agreed. When I got to the meeting, I started to explain my product. Then I took a deep breath and asked the buyer to follow me into the bathroom. At first, she was stunned. But I went into the stall and did my own personal live before-and-after demonstration with my crème-colored pants. When she saw how dramatic the difference was when I put on my Spanx, she wrote an order, and the company was born.

Of course, I was scared to make that initial call. I convinced myself that *I* was doing *her* the favor. I had to trick my brain into thinking this, and after I did, I was no longer afraid of asking and had the confidence to go for it. I asked, and then showed up with the goods. Now I have a multimillion-dollar company, and women everywhere don't have panty lines.

—SARA BLAKELY, *founder and owner, Spanx, Inc.*

She Asked for It!

I had been appearing as a career expert on ABC's *Good Morning America* for several months. The feedback on my segments from the producers and viewers was consistently positive, and I continued to be invited back.

Often people would ask me if I was a contributor to the show, which is an official designation reserved for various experts who appear regularly on the program.

Each time I would have to say no. Even though I was doing a lot of work for these segments, I didn't have an official affiliation. I realized that I wasn't much of a career expert if I didn't apply my own advice, which was to ask for the title I deserved.

I asked the executive producer to recognize my work with this distinction, and he said yes immediately. I got the title and the money that were afforded to the other professionals who were doing the same work.

—TORY JOHNSON, CEO, Women For Hire, and workplace contributor,
ABC's *Good Morning America*

clout that comes along with a more senior title. Maybe you think it'll push you into the next pay grade.

Consider why you deserve a better title. This will be the basis for your argument to your employer.

- You've found that clients would rather deal with someone who's more senior. If your title of manager was bumped up to that of director, you're confident that you'd be more effective in resolving disputes with customers and gaining their confidence at the same time.

- As an assistant you do just as much work—sometimes more—than your coworker who has the title of coordinator. You'd like equal billing as a fair and accurate reflection of your responsibilities and contributions.

- Money is tight in your company, and there's no talk of annual raises. Even though it's not as meaningful as more cash, you want a more senior title as a sign of appreciation for your work.

If more money is your main motive in seeking a new title, be aware of three things:

1. You'll be expected to do more and achieve bigger results with this new title. Know ahead of time what you're getting yourself into and whether it's worth the effort, energy, and possible sacrifices.

2. If you're straining under financial burdens and they are driving your request, make certain you do not relay this to your employer. It's not the boss's problem, nor are such troubles justification for a raise or a new title.

3. Although more money is always important, there are other benefits that may emerge from a better title, and these should not be overlooked. Don't be blinded by money so that you wind up overlooking other perks that may be meaningful to your career. For example, your new title might entitle you to attend key meetings or weigh in on important business decisions.

Have a clear vision. The time you spend with your boss will need to be well thought out in advance. Not only should you prepare talking points as to why you deserve this new title, but you'll want to address how this promotion fits into the organization as a whole.

Timing is everything, and a great time to win a new title is at the end of a salary negotiation. Negotiate at a time when your value to the company is high. Adjust your strategy based on what the economy is doing, but act when your own stock is up. And always try to tie your request to the company's bottom line. You should also consider asking for a new title when your workload increases, the company is being restructured, or you have greater visibility with outside clients.

When suggesting a new title, it's important to consider office politics. Is there a clear reporting structure? Then try creating a title outside of current descriptions. For example, if a director reports to a vice president, she shouldn't ask for a VP title. Instead, she should ask for "senior director" or "group director." This enables her to achieve a higher position without diminishing the supervisor's role.

When the time comes, walk into the meeting and confidently explain why you're asking for the new title and why you deserve it. If there are obvious benefits to the company, make them known. For example, if you've gotten another offer, you may be able to leverage it to get a more prestigious title at your current company. The benefit to them is being able to retain you. If you're in a sales or customer-relations role, you can easily argue that a better title will give you more clout with key constituents and thus improve efficiency and increase sales for the company. Your argument might also be that giving you the better title is the right and fair thing to do, which may also be enough justification for an employer, so long as you've earned the title.

Bring a brag folder. Employers are usually more open to requests from those who exceed their job descriptions. Your brag folder should contain information that documents your accomplishments. You should include:

- *Recent list of achievements*—peak sales, early quotas met or exceeded, and company improvements you were involved in and the resulting savings or efficiency enhancements

- *Additional responsibilities*—those tasks or projects you either inherited or volunteered for

- *Advanced education*—training, certification, or degrees that you acquired during your employment at the company

- *Letters of commendation*—thank-you notes from clients bosses, direct reports, or peers that verify your efforts and results

If your request is rejected, ask what exactly you would need to accomplish to be awarded the new title you seek. Leave the meeting with a resolution, some solutions, or a few next steps with a definitive timetable. Your boss may need to see you perform at a higher level before giving you the title. Know what the issues are, and then establish a time frame for revisiting them. If the boss suggests next year, you might counter with the possibility of 5 months rather than 12. Make it clear that you will be following up in the agreed-upon time frame and addressing any issues that need to be dealt with in the interim. In this way you create a record of the negotiation and will be able to have a targeted meeting in the future.

After the meeting, write up the terms you agreed to—what goals you have to achieve within the time frame specified by your boss—and e-mail them to him for final confirmation. Any good manager

She Asked for It!

I had been in the television industry in Salt Lake City for about two years when the station hired me as a general-assignment reporter. I was the youngest person at that station and among the youngest in the market.

After I'd been on the job for eight months, the morning anchor position opened up, and I would have killed for it. Those openings don't come around often, and when they do, everyone wants them.

All of the anchors and reporters who were older than me put their hats in the ring. I didn't think I was worthy to put my name in the running. I knew if I had the job, I'd succeed, but an overwhelming feeling of shyness and intimidation kept me from giving it a shot.

A colleague at the station came to me and quietly suggested that I reconsider. After that boost, I went into our news director, and I asked to be considered for the spot. She told me she was glad I had changed my mind, and she gave me the position.

I signed a three-year contract as the morning anchor, and was then promoted to a larger market, which is where I am today.

—MEGAN HENDERSON, anchor, Fox's *Good Day Dallas*

would want to encourage you to meet those goals and would then reward you accordingly.

How to Ask for More Responsibility

If you are making this request and we're your boss, we like you already. Anyone thinking about how she can contribute more to an organization already has the attitude that most employers want. Your desire to do more work should be met with great enthusiasm, which will be justified if you do it well.

There are many different reasons you'd approach your manager with such a request. You're bored with your current tasks, you don't feel challenged in your position, or you have too much free time once everything is completed. This last reason takes a big person to admit, but doing so certainly shows honesty and ambition.

Your rationale could also be entirely on the other end of the spectrum. You may be completely satisfied with what you do and strongly committed to your company's well-being, but you're interested in taking on an additional task in order to expand your capabilities while contributing to the company's success.

ARE YOU READY? How do you know if and when you're ready for more work? Only you really know for certain. Not only will your boss ask this question, but also, more importantly, you need to ask it of yourself. Getting in over your head is usually worse than not taking on any more work at all.

- Can you handle your present assignments with ease, factoring in the occasional unpredictable problems and mishaps?

- Do you have the mental and emotional stability to handle the additional stress that goes with a larger workload?

- Will you be able to cope with a new set of critiques from the boss and possibly other coworkers?

- Are you willing to give up personal time, perhaps without additional compensation at the onset? Seeking and accepting more work doesn't mean you're entitled to an immediate raise. In some cases, especially when your employer requests that you substantially increase your workload, you may be offered an increase. However, you'll be able to use these new responsibilities and accomplishments as ammunition for a raise, bonus, or promotion during your annual review.

- Do you have the necessary skills? Don't assume that your boss has the time or inclination to train you if what you're asking for requires acquiring additional skills or knowledge. You'll be more successful if, before approaching your boss, you have already figured out how you will acquire the skills or tackle the project.

Know exactly what you are asking for, even if you don't know exactly what you want. For example, are you asking for a specific assignment that you have your eyes on, or are you asking for more work in general? Besides knowing what to specifically ask for, be prepared to say why you are asking for it. That might be the boss's biggest concern since nobody wants you to take on more than you can handle. Tell your manager something like, "I've learned my job very well, and I've actually figured out how to do some things in a more efficient way; I'm ready to do more. I'd like you to consider letting me service an additional account, take calls from another region, or add the Patterson project to my plate."

Another scenario might be a request to work on a high-profile project outside of your normal scope. Such work could help you to gain valuable new skills or to raise your own profile among key constituents in your company. In such a case you'd want to make it clear that you're willing to work longer hours for this opportunity, and that you are confident your regular work will remain up to par. "Since our consumer-products division is unveiling a new line next season, I'd welcome the chance to be involved in the event-planning activities surrounding the launch. I am prepared to maintain my current workload while taking on additional tasks and responsibilities since the experience would expand my skills and knowledge. I would be a great asset to the team in charge, and I'm hoping you'll be willing to help facilitate this."

If you are seeking this additional work with an eye toward moving laterally or being promoted, consider discussing your career development with your manager. Do not reveal that motive to your manager at this time. Show your commitment to your current role and express a desire to grow professionally with the company.

DO IT INSTEAD OF ASKING. Another alternative to getting more responsibility is to do something that needs to be done without waiting to be asked, while being careful to respect protocol and not step on someone else's toes. This demonstrates your ambition, commitment, and professional ethics. Although your everyday tasks should be done completely and well, you should volunteer for other jobs you know will challenge you.

Contributor: Carolyn N. Turknett, coauthor of *Decent People, Decent Company: How to Lead with Character at Work and in Life*

She Asked for It!

I regret not asking to participate in a presentation at a major conference that was being hosted by the institution I was consulting for. I did not ask to participate because I was intimidated by the credentials of the other presenters (all holding doctorates), as well as the credentials of the audience (all medical doctors). My highest formal degree was a Master of Arts, although I had completed more-advanced studies, had a wide range of clinical experience, and had done graduate study in supervision and administration. Because I did not ask, the institution hired a doctoral-level professional in my field to present. I felt resentful and unimportant, and my ability to interact with my colleagues at work suffered as a result.

The next time the opportunity arose, I selected a novel topic that I knew would be of interest to the administration, and then I requested a chance to participate. Because they had never heard me present, yet were familiar with my performance at work, they gave me a shortened amount of time to speak at the conference. I fully researched the topic, compiled a well-planned and sophisticated presentation, and practiced it extensively. As a result, my presentation went smoothly, and I was very well received.

The only regret expressed to me was that they had not allowed me more time in the program. At the following conference, I was given equal time, which made me feel that I had earned the respect of my peers.

—BETTY SUNSHINE, CEO, Sunshine Speech and Language Services

How to Ask for Recognition

An extremely important part of managing your career is getting the recognition due to you. As women, we tend to downplay our successes for fear of appearing conceited. And while it's true that bragging excessively is obnoxious and frowned upon, that doesn't mean you should stop short of taking credit for your work—and seeking credit, too, at every stage of your career.

For example, a vice president successfully executes a shareholder meeting, and the CEO seeks her out to offer his compliments. He says, "Excellent job. The event came off without a hitch." She should say, "I appreciate your recognition of my efforts. A lot of work went into planning this event. I'm delighted that all the preparation paid off for everyone." She should never bashfully say, "Oh, it was nothing" simply because she is too shy and intimidated to accept the credit and praise. This is precious recognition that she has received from the CEO, and it can lead to raises and promotions if she seizes it and uses it wisely.

While nobody should expect a pat on the back for every little thing they do well, sometimes it's advisable to ask for recognition even when it's not offered. When you achieve a major task at work, go to your boss and say, "I'm very proud of my contribution to the shareholder meeting last week. I was thrilled to play an important role in such a successful event. It would mean a lot to me if you included my contribution in your weekly report to senior management." Your boss should be willing to do this on your behalf, and when it's done, be certain to express your appreciation. You are documenting your contribution and making it known to key decision makers.

- Request this right after the project has been successfully completed.

- Ask for this when you have made a clear-cut contribution.

- Ask for recognition like this at least three to four times a year, or more often if major accomplishments warrant it.

- Always be direct about what you want in the way of recognition.

A BOSS WHO HESITATES TO SHARE CREDIT. You may have a boss who is reluctant to share credit. She may worry about being perceived negatively. In this case, phrase your question differently. When you ask to be recognized, say, "Because of the direction and support that you gave to me, I was able to achieve this." Or, "Because of the support, direction, and motivation that you provide, I was able to achieve this particular success. I'm hoping that you will find the opportunity to share that with senior management." Offer to write a statement that she can forward. It should give her credit as your manager and detail your own contributions as well.

You can also frame your request by saying, "Since this company is driven by results, my growth is entirely dependent on the results of my own performance. Because of that, I know it's important for all of us to document our contributions. I'm hoping that as my manager you will be willing to give me the credit I deserve for the projects I complete."

Keep a log of your successes. You should date the entries and list the specific work you accomplished. Make note of anyone who would vouch for your contributions.

Any time a colleague or client sends you a note of thanks—"We appreciate your work on this project" or "Your contributions saved the day"—be sure to print out copies and put them in your own "me" file. Similarly, if a colleague or client calls to offer the same recognition, thank him or her for the kind words and record it in your own journal. Since annual reviews, raises, bonuses, and promotions are all based on performance, this information will come in handy during those key conversations.

Put your company newsletter to work for you. Contact the editor and say, "I know that our newsletter celebrates the accomplishments of our employees. For the next issue, I hope you might consider a news item on me. I just won an award for a campaign I completed on behalf of our company this year. It's the most prestigious award in my field. Can I send you some information?" If anyone else on your team contributed to the success, be sure to include his or her role as well. You will appear selfish if you focus completely on yourself if in fact other people were key contributors as well. You may also choose to seek recognition outside the company by working with the local media and trade press, particularly when your job is to win external accounts.

How to Ask to Review Your Personnel File

There may be times at work when you sense that trouble is brewing. You believe that someone may have reprimanded you unfairly. If you work for a large company, this type of action can become part of your personnel file. Negative items such as poor performance appraisals or written reprimands can prevent you from being promoted, or even lead to your dismissal if you demonstrate the same behaviors repeatedly. They also can be used as criteria for dismissing you if there is a reduction in force (RIF), or downsizing.

She Asked for It!

In the early years, the hardest thing for me to do was ask for recognition and what I'd call applause. I felt my work should speak for itself and win recognition on its own. I found out that you have to toot your own horn—respectfully, not boastfully. You also must declare your goal to the person you want to recognize you: "I want to be recognized as your number-one rep. I want to go on the recognition trip." Declare it early and go back often to see how you are doing in regard to that goal.

—KAREN DONNALLEY, director of sales, Software, Americas IBM.com

When you ask to see your file, remain calm and unemotional since you do not want to exacerbate what may already be a tense situation. Asking to see your file is often viewed as a defensive action and alerts the other party to your concern. Ask by approaching your human-resources contact and saying, "I'd like to schedule a convenient time to review the contents of my personnel file. Are you the correct person to accommodate this request?"

Most employees have no idea what's in their files. But if you work for a large corporation, you almost definitely have one. Your personnel file is a collection of information that paints a picture of you, and people will judge you based on its contents. When you look through it, you will likely see:

- Your application

- Your offer letter

- Your résumé

- Your job description

- Performance evaluations

- Development records (training, education, and degrees)

- Special awards and commendation letters

- Disciplinary letters

- Time and attendance records

Your access to your personnel file may be limited in your area since laws vary from state to state. In addition, employment laws may govern what may be contained in your official personnel file. Your supervisor may also maintain an unofficial file where he or she keeps notes about your performance throughout the year.

If you work for a small business, you may be more direct about your intent. Say, "I have some concerns over what may be included in my file. Could I please review it for a few moments?" In this type of setting, you can sometimes discuss your concerns more informally.

In some states, you are not allowed to remove any items from the file—even if you believe errors exist. But in some states, you are allowed to amend the information by submitting your own explanation and specifically asking that it be placed in your permanent file. End the letter by saying, "Please include this letter in my personnel file."

You may have a right to copy the contents of your file, although your employer may charge you a copying fee. There are generally certain items that may not belong in your official personnel file, which may include:

- Preemployment references/background checks

- Grievances

- Outside agency complaints

- Affirmative-action data

- I-9 documentation

- Credit reports

- Documents related to injury or disability

If you find any of these items, you may have a right to ask for them to be removed.

How to Ask to Switch Departments Within a Company

There are different reasons for wanting an overall change. You could have a serious interest in a new department, having maxed out your talents in your current position. You may be bored with your current position, which is no longer stimulating your intellect. Maybe the problem is the people you work with, and you'd like to surround yourself with another team. Cut to the core of your desire.

For example, a publicist in network news wants to switch fields and become a producer or booker for a specific television show because she's grown tired of her day-to-day responsibilities. She has simultaneously gained a strong interest in the editorial side of the operation. She could very well stay with the same employer, but transfer to another department.

A public-relations executive at a major agency might want to shift from handling communications in the technology sector to handling communications for a nonprofit organization. She wants to apply the same skills and experience to a different type of client, which requires a change in department or a reassignment of her accounts.

For you it may just be a matter of changing from floor 6 to floor 10 in order to shift from sales to human resources within the same company and possibly reinvigorate your career. In any of these situations, how do you lay out your plan to move?

Assess exactly why you want a change and list the pros and cons of staying where you are and moving on. After three years in your current position, you quite possibly will have learned most everything you want or need to know. If gaining new knowledge is your goal, then changing roles will give you a greater opportunity to do so.

Are you willing to overcome the roadblocks or defy the naysayers who encourage you to stay put? The change must really be worth it to you since you'll have to persevere to make it happen.

APPROACH THE CHANGE EFFECTIVELY. Since you can't just announce to your boss that you're miserable and want to switch departments, you should start by learning how transfers are typically initiated within your company. Usually businesses welcome an internal transfer if you are a good performer with a strong work history. In fact, before accepting external applications, large companies often post job openings internally to allow current employees to make their interests known. First speak with your manager about your desire to change. Explain how much you appreciate everything you've learned and why it's time for you to move on. "I've learned a great deal working with you. At this stage, I've contributed as much as I can to this department, and I think it's time for me to move into an area where I can continue to develop new skills and create successes for the company. Might you be agreeable to helping me make such a transition?" This shows respect for the person in charge of your work and prevents the creation of tension or animosity later.

If you then receive no assistance and only get ignored, consult with human resources and possibly the head of the department you would like to join. Let them know that you tried first to involve your boss since you don't want to be viewed as someone who's disgruntled or attempting an underhanded move. You want to maintain harmony as best you can, so be pleasant and respectful of everyone involved.

SAY IT CORRECTLY. What do you say when asking to transfer? Identify your transferable skills, and talk up your contributions to your current department as well as the depth of your knowledge of the organization. Since the company will be losing a person in one department, show who and what it will be gaining in another. Sometimes it's better for a company to accommodate your request to transfer than to risk losing you since the cost and hassle of turnover are considerable. Facilitating internal moves is also an advantage to the company because the moves can be timed to allow for ample training of your replacement and a smooth transition all around.

Receiving a transfer on your first request is by no means guaranteed. While the company may very well value your talents, another applicant might fit the role better. If the company rejects your request, ask why it did so. Find out what it will take for such a transfer to be approved and when you should revisit this issue. You might not have the specific skill-set that the department you want to move into is looking for. If that's the case, ask the company to provide the necessary training either internally or through outside courses so that you'll be eligible when another comparable opening comes along.

Other times you'll be passed over because the head of the department you want to join doesn't know you. To develop a rapport with that manager, offer to serve on committees or participate in programs that might give you the opportunity to interact with him. You should also figure out how to get to know the people within that department, since they are likely to have the boss's ear. Find out how their department operates. Get a feel for the general vibe among the staff members and for their overall satisfaction level. This could increase your desire to join that new group, or it could raise concerns that will make you think twice about making a move. If you get the sense that the move would be right for you, you now have specific internal connections and can make your professional desires known.

Make certain that any new position you go for will challenge you and satisfy you, not only in terms of position and salary, but also in terms of growth and goals. Don't move to get away from one boss before you've had a chance to get to know the style of the prospective new boss. Resist the urge to make a switch until you've done all of your homework and are clear about what you're getting into.

How to Ask Your Boss to Share More Information

Some supervisors communicate very little. Getting anything out of them can be like pulling teeth. They are only vocal when they're upset or you've crossed a line.

The way to avoid such missteps is to cultivate an open relation-

She Asked for It!

Right after journalism school, I started at a position where I was a part-time freelancer, hired to write headlines and captions at a major newspaper. I was really excited to get the gig, but my goal was to write feature-length articles.

A few weeks into the job, after I felt like I'd settled in a bit, I had a conversation with the editor and made it known that I'd love to pitch her ideas and write for the section as long as it didn't take away from my other duties. She said, "Pitch away!" Within a few weeks, I had my first article in the features section—and ever since, I've written features regularly.

It was such a simple conversation to have, but a challenge for me—I always used to think that people would automatically assume I wanted to write and that I was talented enough or intelligent enough to do the job.

It was one of my first lessons: so few things will fall into your lap, and if you want something, you have to raise your hand and ask for it. And if at first you don't get what you want, just keep raising your hand. And never stop asking.

—MACKENZIE DAWSON, editor, *New York Post*

ship with your supervisor in which you feel comfortable encouraging conversation. You want to strive for "transparency"—a relationship built on honesty, clarity, and trust. In some cases, especially those involving managers who keep things close to the vest, the burden falls on you to create a good relationship. It might not be possible to get your boss to open up overnight, but your commitment to pursuing an ongoing dialogue will ultimately generate the results you're in search of.

Always look to grasp the big picture in the workplace and to work with your boss to understand it. Keep in mind that your manager has limited time and may also be privy to confidential information that cannot be shared with his team, so be wise about what you're asking.

Look for problems at work that can be resolved with better communication. For example, you may have just finished an assignment for the director of your department, only to discover that the work—your work—was ultimately intended for the CEO. Had you known this, you would have done things differently—from using better paper and avoiding shorthand notes to providing a summary of results.

In this case, you might say to your boss, "It would help me in the future to precisely understand the intended use of a project. This may affect the information I choose to include in a report and the manner in which it is prepared. Had I known that report was for the CEO, I would have presented it more formally and with greater detail." It is important to keep this dialogue free of emotion. You may follow up a conversation by reiterating your concerns in a letter. Say, "Thanks for discussing this with me today. It's been my experience that when I'm kept out of the loop, I can't operate as effectively as I should. I need to know the full context for the project, so that I can properly develop the content that I include in my reports."

PURSUE QUESTIONS, GET ANSWERS. A good time to ask is at the beginning of an assignment. For example, your boss may announce that your team is going to undertake a major inventory research project. He assigns tasks and establishes expectations. It is not unreasonable for you to ask why this work is being done and how it fits into the larger scope of the company. You can say, "I'm clear about my role in this project, but I'm hoping you'll be willing to share with us how the project came to be. I'd also like to know its intended purpose since that might impact our methodology and presentation." When you use this approach, you are acknowledging what needs to be done, and you're asking for something in exchange. Hopefully this will make your boss more receptive to sharing information.

Appeal to the rational side of your supervisor. Try different methods to get him or her to open up and share information. For example, some people will be more honest and informative in e-mail. They write very well, and find e-mail a safe way to communicate. In this case, a well-thought-out e-mail may produce the information you desire. For example, "I've been brainstorming ways to deliver the results of our research findings, and I'd like to know for whom this information is intended and how exactly it will be used once we complete it. This knowledge will help me to present it in the ideal format for its audience."

Another method is to say, "I don't have the benefit of the full picture, because I don't attend meetings like you do. I find that my work is much stronger and more thorough when I have that understanding. Would you be willing to share the notes from the monthly management meeting you participate in?" You can also point to ways that you would intend to put that knowledge and information to use. For example, "To improve customer service, it would be beneficial for me to know the feedback you are getting from our top clients. Would you share with me the daily status reports you receive?"

In cases in which your boss is simply not meeting your need for more information, be direct but stay polite and respectful. Say, "I had asked you about the purpose of the inventory report while I was working on it last week. You implied you wanted a cursory report, which is why I requested that level of detail from you. My understanding now is that we needed more-detailed information for the head of the company. Had I known that, I would have handled the report differently. Would you please tell me why you didn't share this information with me last week?"

If your initial requests for information fail, do not give up. Continue to ask questions and solicit information from your manager. You may have to vary your questions or even your timing to elicit the responses you desire, but don't abandon your mission.

How to Ask for Feedback on an Idea Without Losing Credit

When you think you've come up with a great idea, you will generally be tempted to run them past coworkers before sharing them with your boss. While most coworkers are trusting team members, the risk is having someone take your ideas and present them as his or her own. While we'd all like to think this won't happen, sadly it does. There are times to be a team player, and other times when it's important to guard your ideas, and present them to decision makers to ensure you receive proper credit for them. Many workers are under pressure in today's economy, and everyone is trying to hold onto their jobs. A good idea—something "outside the box"—is just the plum someone might be looking to snatch.

The best way to handle this is to acknowledge the realities of the workplace. Learn to rely on your instinct and trust your own judgment. Put your idea into writing. This way, you will have a paper trail fully developing it and proving that you didn't just plant the

She Asked for It!

A lot of times we don't ask for what we want—not because we are afraid to ask, but because we're afraid that if we get what we want, we may not be able to deliver. You have to be willing to put yourself on the line and push through the fear and try. I found that I always did better at delivering than I thought I would. When you succeed, it gives you the confidence to ask for something much harder and much bigger next time.

You have to also be ready to not get what you want. Part of what you must ask yourself is, *What's the worst possible thing that could happen?* The women who never fail are the women who never ask for anything and instead sit back waiting for things—which ultimately never happen.

—LYN TURKNETT, president, Turknett Leadership Group

seed, but thought the idea through and really invested yourself. This often also means giving nothing away for free, unless doing so is part of your job description or the culture of your work environment and contractually expected of you, which is sometimes the case.

Still, you need to manage the risk of presenting an idea when it's to your favor to get credit, which means figuring out the safest way to ask for feedback. After all, a big idea can either go over brilliantly, or it can fail brilliantly. And you want to avoid embarrassing yourself at an important meeting. One solution is to look to people outside your department for feedback. These people may be mentors, trusted coworkers in other departments, friends at other companies, or trusted peers in your industry.

Say, for example, you are an editor at a magazine aimed at professional women. The magazine's main focus is fashion and lifestyle, and doesn't directly address work issues. You want to suggest to the editor-in-chief and publisher the idea of refocusing the content or spinning off a new magazine altogether. If you chat about it around the office, you may risk losing credit for the idea.

Instead, you should ask a small group of trusted colleagues outside of your workplace who fit the demographic, "How would you feel about a magazine that addresses your issues at work? The magazine would cover stories on women who have reached the pinnacle of their industries, and it would share information on how they did it."

Trust your instinct about whom to ask. Your most trusted peers are the ones who tell it to you straight without sugarcoating it. Look at any well-balanced, successful professional woman, and you will see that she has a trusted circle of respected professional friends supporting her.

When you ask the right people, you can also gain confidence in your idea. Consider building that feedback right into your presentation. Talk about comments you have received. When you have a big idea, you never want to be tentative about it. Asking for feedback can be an important component of a successful presentation. For example, "The CEO of one of our city's largest privately held, woman-owned businesses, says that many of the issues that her mother confronted in the workplace are still alive and well today. She says we need a resource to help women work smart. We bring unique gifts to the workplace, and we need to learn to thrive—on our own terms."

Instead of soliciting feedback from internal coworkers, you can do research on your idea to see if anything similar already exists or if something similar has previously failed.

In other cases, when the issues are smaller, you may simply choose to keep your ideas to yourself until you are ready to present them. If your own judgment is solid, you don't need feedback. For example, you may be writing a story on identity theft for a magazine. You learn, through doing a series of interviews, that the individual cases are extremely compelling. There is a lot of drama, big financial issues are involved, and oftentimes there is little in the way of closure. After making these points to your editor at a weekly planning meeting, you can add, "How would you feel about making this a future cover? If you are agreeable, we could incorporate additional stories covering this issue from a variety of angles."

Resist the urge to share this information with colleagues ahead of time, especially when you are working in a very competitive environment. You have done your own research, and you don't really need other opinions or advice at this stage. The excitement that you are experiencing is sufficient. You know you have a good idea. This is a time when you need to trust your own judgment. In a competitive arena, feedback will rarely be free of any agenda. In the workplace, information is power.

How to Ask to Transfer to a New City

There are different reasons why you may want to request a transfer to a new city where you can take on a new role or continue in your current one. Some of these reasons are strictly personal, and others are tied to professional advancement. Perhaps the lights of the big city are shouting your name, and you're eager to shake things up and answer the call. For example:

- You want to be closer to your family. It could be that someone is ill or elderly, and you want to be nearer to her or him.

She Asked for It!

When I was a producer at a local television station, I learned that a major new long-term initiative was being planned. Another person had been assigned to handle the project.

I immediately envisioned all of the possibilities for the project and took the weekend to write up my thoughts on the direction that it should take in order to be a win-win for viewers, sponsors, and the station.

After I submitted my ideas in writing and had a follow-up meeting, it was determined that I should spearhead the project. It became a highly successful effort, and now—years afterward—elements of it are still in place. It was a challenge because I had to ask management to reconsider their initial plans. The whole experience taught me that boldness, passion, and enthusiasm can pay off. Nothing is cast in stone.

—DEIDRE MCDONALD, faculty, Clark Atlanta University

- Your spouse has been offered a new job and wants to relocate.

- You want a total change of pace. Whether you are single, married, or divorced, a change of environment is what you need.

- Your current employer is opening an office in a new city, and you want a transfer within the company so that you can get in on the ground floor and help them build and grow.

- You're interested in different work within the same company or a different company that is located in a different city.

FINANCIAL CONSIDERATIONS. Since considerable expenses are likely to be involved, you must first determine if the move means enough for you to pay for it completely on your own. If you're willing to foot the entire bill, research all of the costs by requesting estimates from reputable moving companies based on the contents of your home and the distance between your city and the place you want to move to. A car is an additional expense in moving. You will also incur costs in visiting the other city to secure housing. Knowing whether or not you can afford all of this will affect how you will approach current or prospective employers.

If your current employer is to cover the cost of relocating you to the new city, you must explain to them why it's important to you that they do so and how such support would be beneficial to them. You might say that if they don't support your transfer, you'll leave the company entirely. If you're a top performer or have an in-demand skill-set, then the company will save money by assisting you rather than losing you. But don't threaten to leave unless you absolutely intend to follow through. It is also possible that the position in your target location is vacant and is a higher priority than the one you would be leaving. The company will see you as filling the bigger need, their loss will be less, and more goals will be met—especially if you already know the job.

"I know that our company is opening a new branch in Seattle. My mother lives there and has been battling cancer for the last year. Personally, I believe it's time for me to be near her, especially since the cross-country trips from New York each month are exhausting. Professionally I know I could make a big difference in Seattle, especially since our VP is intent on increasing our business in that region. I'm ready to pack up, jump in, and give it all I've got. Would you be willing to help make this happen?"

Even though this is your request, and not theirs, you can still ask for relocation expenses. (See the chapter on How to Ask for a Relocation Package and Moving Expenses.) There may be pay differentials. Your employer should not be offended if you bring this to their attention, along with other details about the move that concern you.

If you are a store manager for a major retail chain in Miami and you're eyeing a transfer to Chicago, it is less likely that your current employer will pay for the move. They might, however, guarantee you a transfer so that you have a job lined up and ready to go once you relocate. That can be just as important to you, especially if you can keep the costs down or if your spouse's employer is covering the expenses.

If you must travel to have an in-person interview with a prospective employer, it is entirely appropriate for you to request that they pay for your travel expenses—airline ticket, hotel, meals and ground transportation. Some employers will just suggest that you give them a call "when you're in the area"—meaning you will be responsible for the expenses. At that point, you must decide if it's worth it to make a special trip on your own dime to meet with them.

If you are job-searching from a distance, keep in mind that some employers will disqualify you from consideration if they are concerned about relocation costs. This is especially true for easy-to-fill positions. The more senior the role or the more competitive the position, the more likely the company will pay to move you if they desire your services. To avoid having your current location held against you, take your address off your résumé or use the address of a friend in the new area. If you are willing to cover your own expenses, make that clear on your résumé and in your cover letter. You can still make relocation an issue for negotiation if and when you receive an offer.

Before forming any definite plans, develop a strategy for relocating. Have the local newspaper of the city you're eyeing delivered to your current residence or visit it daily online. This will help you to understand the climate, culture, and major issues impacting the city. You'll know the leading economic drivers and the troubling weaknesses in business. Plan to make a couple of trips to get to know the area before deciding to make it your new home. Make a budget that takes into account the actual move, estimated housing costs, climate and cultural differences, education for your children, the timing and planning of advance trips for interviewing, house-hunting, move-in, and other factors. Focus on building a small network to assist you in tapping into personal and professional connections who may help you get established.

How to Ask the Boss to Help You Find a New Job

As surprising as it might sound, your current boss may be your very best resource as you search for a new job. There are often times when a present situation is just not an ideal match, even though the boss has been one of your best advocates and you love working for her. Just because you wish to leave that job doesn't mean you have to do so in an adversarial fashion. If you are honest with your boss and handle your reasons for leaving appropriately, then it's possible to solicit support from her as you move forward in your career. Begin by first asking yourself these questions:

She Should've Asked for It!

Early in my communications career, there was a question I failed to ask. I worked for a small radio station in Portsmouth, New Hampshire. When it was time to contemplate a job in a major market, I thought only about the commute to Boston, which was an hour and a half from my home. I was pregnant at the time, and the combination of considerable distance and pregnancy convinced me not to pursue radio jobs in Boston. I failed to ask myself if there was another way. Perhaps there was a midmarket I might have entered. Maybe I needed to relocate. Perhaps there were viable options in TV that would not have required the commute, but that would still have represented advancement in the field. The lesson, which I have learned many times over since that time, is to picture the desired end result and find a strategy to get there.

—EVIE SACKS, principal, Evelyn Sacks Communications, Inc.

WHY DO I WANT TO GO? Maybe you've outgrown your current position. Maybe your strengths don't mirror the needs of that position, but would serve another role quite well. Instead of losing you, your company would prefer to transfer you to another department. Maybe it's just time to move on because you need a change of pace. Regardless, a great way to move up and on is to gain the endorsement of your boss. If you respect each other, this will be much better than seeking your options behind her back.

If you have an excellent relationship with your boss and she is a big supporter of your work, then there's a good chance that she will recognize, as you do, that you've done everything possible in your current role and that it's time for you to seek new challenges. The first step is asking to have a candid discussion. Explain how much you appreciate everything you've learned and why it's time to make a change. "I've learned so much working for and with you. At this stage, I've contributed as much as I can to this department, and I think it's time for me to move into an area where I can continue to develop new skills and create successes for this company. Might you be agreeable to helping me make such a transition?"

WHERE CAN I GO? You can explain where you're interested in moving to within the company. As the manager of Customer Care, you've learned every facet of the position and understand how your department intermingles with the other departments, and now you want to aim for an opening as the director of sales. Your current boss knows you have the necessary drive and abilities, as well as a solid track record of successes. It would make all the difference if she stated as much in a direct call to the VP.

Besides, you have a friend who's in a position similar to yours in a different company, and who is also looking for a change. Suggesting that this friend could take your place, and and that you should train her, would certainly be a way to recompense your boss for the favor she did you. Out of respect for both parties, ask for and agree to confidentiality for the entire process.

Your boss could be well connected in your field and could even help you excel outside the company. For example: You've been doing sales in the technology industry, but now you're looking to do sales in the financial arena. She might be willing to help you make the transition since she knows many people in finance.

If you have a good relationship with your boss, are able to discuss some options for your new job, and can assist her in return (by training new employees or staying late to get projects completed), you will enhance the respect between you and have a situation that is ideal for both sides.

What if you don't have a specific job in mind for yourself? You will want to ask your boss to help you identify opportunities to leverage the talents and strengths you possess. If you want a change and don't know how to go about it, and you confide in her about your feelings, you are showing how much you trust her. Just make sure you do have that trust. Once you reveal to your boss you want something "else" or "more," the truth is out. There's no turning back.

WHEN CAN I GO? When asking your boss for help with a new job, try to establish a time frame. Don't let it be an open-ended issue. If it's October and you are looking to leave in 90 days, then that's the goal. If it's 3 weeks, then stick to that plan. Otherwise, everyday events tend to happen, and you and your boss may get caught in the tide and stay there—especially if she doesn't really want you to leave.

You don't have to immediately get all the answers about finding a new job, but figure out the next steps: when you'll meet again for an update; how to tackle the search. Again, offer to help identify a replacement, especially if your boss seems hesitant in letting you go, and express great gratitude for her help.

How to Ask for a Better Severance Package

While bigwig corporate executives often walk away with millions of dollars in severance, most of us wind up pocketing several weeks or months of pay, if that, when our employment ends.

A severance package is an offer of compensation, benefits, property, or services made to an employee who has been terminated without cause, perhaps due to a reorganization or restructuring, company sale or merger, or cost-cutting initiative. Although severance packages may not be required by law, many employers may provide them in exchange for a guarantee from their employees not to sue, defame the company or otherwise tarnish its reputation, and—in many cases—not to join the competition or start a competing operation.

While a package can take many shapes and forms, the most common elements include cash (severance pay, payment for accrued vacation, stock options), extended medical coverage, use of company property (company car, laptop, cell phone), and outplacement services (résumé writing, letters of reference, job training, technology resources, workshops, coaching, job leads).

By asking for a better severance package than the one you've been offered, you run the risk that the company will infer that you are rejecting its initial offer. If your employer denies your counterproposal, they may not allow you to accept their original offer.

If you are part of a mass layoff, your bargaining power is far less than if you are terminated independently. Large downsizings require significant planning, and by the time they are announced, severance packages have been determined and organizations may have decided not to make exceptions for specific employees.

The best way to start the process of asking for an enhanced package is to consider two strategies:

- Ask yourself which aspects of the package are acceptable and which are not. Carefully examine your employer's initial offer and identify the areas you would like to see enhanced.

- Ask the experts. You should consider getting professional legal opinion on the terms, language, and other details of the agreement before signing it.

Do not allow your superiors, the human-resources department, or any other managers within the company to pressure you into quickly accepting the offer. Ask for a deadline. Typically, employers will give you at least a couple weeks to make a decision. The amount of time you will have in which to evaluate your options and sign an agreement will depend on your age. In addition, you may also receive a window of time in which you can change your mind.

Once you have determined what you consider to be a reasonable goal, schedule a face-to-face meeting with someone in your organization whom you feel comfortable speaking candidly to and who has some influence in the final decision and might be willing to lobby for you. Convince this person that your request is justified by emphasizing:

- Your contributions to the company and your stellar performance record

- Professional and personal sacrifices that you made to join the company

- Any unusual circumstances (economic hardships, family problems, health issues) you have encountered while under the company's employ that you did not allow to affect your exceptional performance

- Any unfair treatment associated with the layoff, especially if you consulted with an employment lawyer who raised this issue.

After you've spelled out exactly what you're asking for, follow up frequently, exude confidence, and be willing to negotiate.

Contributor: Robert Damon, president, North America for Korn/Ferry International

She Asked for It!

I was asked by my company to take on a new position that meant an entirely new career path. It was during a time of change for me. A brand-new mom, I had a newborn at home and felt it was important for me to think of my family's security. For the first time in my career, I had to think of what was best for my family. I was reluctant at first to negotiate further, but I did ask for a severance package in the event that my job was eliminated. Since the company offered me the new position and wanted me to take it on, I felt it was reasonable to make this request. I was extremely appreciative and pleased that they valued me enough to say yes.

—MARY LYNN RYAN, southeast bureau chief, CNN

Successful Networking

How to Ask for General Career Advice

During your career—especially at certain milestones in your advancement—you will come across people whom you will want to meet and learn from. They have crossed barriers that you haven't. They make climbing the corporate ladder look easy. They can help you tap a knowledge base that would take you years to access on your own. You meet these people in a myriad of ways, from giving them praise at work to volunteering with them at a nonprofit fund-raiser. When you ignite a conversation with one of them, instantly creating a dialogue, you discover that there's so much to learn from her experiences, and you want to get to know her.

The pros call this networking, but we simply call it working smart. As your circle of influence grows, you find the value in meeting new people and increasing both whom you know and what you know.

The majority of women at the senior-executive level emphasize the importance of getting good career advice when trying to advance. This can be very different from mentoring, because the person you turn to for a specific piece of career advice might give you enough help in one in-depth conversation; you will not need to form an ongoing, long-term relationship with him or her. You might need immediate assistance with any number of issues, including resolving a conflict with a colleague, delivering a presentation, responding to an offer of a promotion, making an important business decision, delegating responsibilities, or juggling a work-and-family conflict, among many other possibilities.

To begin, ask yourself: how can I approach this person for advice? The challenging part is figuring out whom to approach for help. Focus first on people who have shown an interest in your work. This could be a family friend whom you see once or twice a year at holiday gatherings, but who would be happy to hear from you at other times.

You may also look to people who have a skill-set that you need. A good way to initiate contact is to express interest in them and their work. For example, you could say, "I'm so interested in learning more about your industry and how you've advanced. Perhaps you'd be willing to share some insights with me as well as suggest which organizations I should join."

Look for guidance inside your company. This could come from women or men in positions of responsibility that mirror the path you're hoping to take. Join an internal women's network, if one exists in your company; it could offer a wealth of support.

The person from whom you wish to seek advice might be a stranger. If possible, go hear her speak. You should pose meaningful questions as an audience member. If she is an author, attend her book signing to show interest in her work. Post a book review online about how her book has helped you and e-mail her directly through her Web site; almost all authors have one. Explain the support you've shown for her work and ask if she'd be willing to reciprocate with 15 minutes of advice. Ask to schedule a time by phone or in person at her convenience.

If you read about someone in the press who you believe is particularly knowledgeable in an area where you need advice, send a copy of the story along with a brief letter congratulating him or her on the coverage, detailing your background and request for advice. If your note is well written, there's a chance you'll receive a response.

Other places to look for career advice inside your network include your college alumni association, previous places of employment, and professional organizations.

With everyone you approach, show respect, build rapport, and demonstrate reciprocity. Begin a relationship in the way that feels most comfortable to you. You're not necessarily looking for an ongoing or long-term mentoring type of arrangement. You may simply need specific onetime advice that this person is ideally suited to give you.

How to Ask for an Informational Interview

When you are new to the workforce, informational interviews are an excellent way to expand your network and investigate potential career opportunities. At more-advanced stages in your career, informational interviews—or exploratory meetings—are get-to-know-you conversations that may open up the potential of consulting work, lead to other professional referrals, or lay the groundwork for possible hire when the opportunity arises. An informational interview is not a formal job interview. You are interviewing them, versus their interviewing you. You are not expecting this person to hire you for a specific opening, at least not right now. When you ask for an informational interview, it's important that you adhere to that understanding. You are gathering information about an industry or a company, or about how that person ended up in his or her role.

The world is wide open to you when it comes to scheduling an informational interview. In some cases, you may need to be referred through a third party. You also have free rein to call up someone out of the blue. For the most part, you can ask a person at any level in an organization. The key is how you ask.

STRUCTURING YOUR REQUEST. Don't convey a sense of entitlement. Explain the common connection you share. For example, you and this person may be members of the same industry association. You may have just heard this person speak. Explain the affiliation and who you are. Then make the request. For example, "I heard your speech last week at the event-planning conference. I was very impressed that you have been able to continue to expand your business throughout the recession. I graduated from college this year and am new to the industry. I am hoping you might have a few moments to speak with me about your career path."

BE FLEXIBLE. Give this person a wide window of time in which he can meet with you. If you are available every day after 4:00 P.M., say so. Let the other person choose the date and location that are most convenient for him. Ask if before the meeting he would like you to forward any information on your background and goals. Some people might appreciate this; others might decline because they don't have time to review the information.

Show respect and be flexible, and you are very likely to get the meeting. When you do, treat it in a professional manner. Arrive a few minutes early and be polite and prepared. This could ultimately lead to a job or a valuable referral.

If you didn't have the opportunity to share information about yourself and your goals prior to the meeting, begin the conversation by providing a brief overview of where you are in your career and why this conversation is important to you.

Among the questions you should ask during the meeting are the following: What sparked your initial interest in this line of work? How did you land your positions? What drew you to this company? Do you belong to industry associations, and are there groups that you'd recommend I join? What are the difficulties and challenges facing this field? Where are the opportunities for growth in this industry? What do you look for when making hiring decisions? What additional skills or experience do you think would make me a valuable asset to an employer? Do you have any suggestions for people or resources I should pursue in my current job search? Would it be okay with you if I kept you posted on my search and we stayed in touch?

Remember, you are in control of the informational interview. The other person has no idea what advice you need or what information you might find helpful unless you provide her or him with specific questions and a brief overview of your background and goals.

MIDCAREER PROFESSIONALS. Further along in your career, you will find that the term *informational interview* isn't used as much. Instead, people schedule lunches or meet for drinks to discuss issues of mutual interest in a specific field. However, this by no means precludes you from pursuing informational or exploratory conversations. In fact, the more experience you have to your credit, the more you are likely to have something valuable to offer the person you're seeking to meet. While it is good to seek meetings with senior human-resources professionals about their companies' hiring needs, it is even better to arrange time to meet with the managers of the business units you'd like to join. This requires more research and effort on your part.

Start by reading media coverage, corporate press releases, and industry-specific publications to figure out who's who in the field of your choice. When you come across like-minded individuals, you can call or e-mail any or all of them with your request for a meeting. Be clear up front about what you offer, not just what you're seeking.

WHAT'S IN IT FOR THEM? Quite often, professionals are happy to share their knowledge and experiences. They regard informational interviews as a way of giving back. This is especially true for professionals near retirement. They spent a lifetime acquiring knowledge, and they have a desire to share. At other times, early-to-mid-stage professionals are happy to help because they recently received help from someone else. This is their chance to reciprocate from the other side of the desk. Managers will also agree to informational meetings as a personal favor or professional courtesy.

Many professionals both inside and outside of human resources also see informational interviewing as a way to tap a potential source of new talent. Since the conversations can be more informal than interviews for a specific position, these professionals see a side of a potential candidate that might not ordinarily come across. Agreeing to such meetings is also a way for professionals to keep their hands on the pulse of what people are saying and thinking about their industry. It provides perspective that can often be valuable.

KNOW YOU HAVE SOMETHING TO OFFER. A common mistake that those new to the workforce make is thinking they have nothing to offer at the informational-interview stage. They haven't yet learned to think strategically and professionally. When you request an informational interview, you should share any successes that you've already had, whether it's internship experience, a strong college record, or even impressive volunteer initiatives. In a request for an informational interview at a large technology company, a recent college graduate might include, "I'd be happy to share with you my insights and impressions about how this industry and your company have impacted my peers through the recruitment process on campus." You might offer the names of well-known industry people whom you've worked alongside of who would vouch for your accomplishments. Above all, show passion for the industry and a genuine desire to advance in a particular field. Be sure to write a thank-you note and express your gratitude for the person's time. Remember that everyone wants to help a potential winner, and that a display of professional enthusiasm and gratitude on your end can be contagious.

She Asked for It!

My dream was to open a women's clothing boutique, so I worked for a college friend at her boutique, and I asked questions at every chance—about start-up costs, financing, purchasing, merchandising, location, customer service. I soaked up all of the information and inspiration she had to offer. She opened her books to me and patiently explained step-by-step how I could start my own business.

Now when my customers ask me how I started this business, I realize that if I hadn't asked for help, my dream of opening Lisa Brown Atlanta might have never become reality.

—LISA BROWN, boutique owner

How to Ask for a Reference

References are an excellent way to enhance a résumé and your chances of being hired, so you want your list to be impressive. Think about this at the beginning stages of the interview process—not at the last second, when you're pressed to come up with names.

EARLY YEARS. Internships are an excellent resource for entry-level references. Since most internships tend to pay very little or nothing at all, references—in addition to valuable experience—become your reward. At the end of the internship, you may say, "I really enjoyed working for you. This was a great experience and I feel very good about my contributions. I'm looking forward to applying this knowledge in the future as I launch my career. Would you consider writing a short letter of reference for me, describing my work here and giving your thoughts on my performance?" If a letter isn't possible, you can ask, "Would it be okay for me to use you as a reference going forward? If so, what would you say about me? What contact information would be appropriate for me to share with potential employers?"

Create a folder and accumulate reference letters as well as commendations for a job, well-done. Consider asking more than one person for a letter that addresses your performance, especially if you interacted with many different people and departments.

DURING TIMES OF TRANSITION. Even if you're not in the process of looking for a new job, get in the habit of asking for a letter of reference from someone you have worked with for a period of time who might be thinking of leaving her or his company. This may be a boss or a client contact. Ask this person to write a letter of reference for you on company letterhead. This shows the relationship of the reference writer to your work, and establishes the value of the reference regardless of whether or not the contact actually leaves the company. Begin this request with a compliment, and acknowledge the positive relationship you've had. You can say, "I've really enjoyed working for you, and your guidance and support have been invaluable to me. I also feel great about the successes I've contributed to our joint projects. Would you mind sharing your thoughts about our professional relationship in a letter of reference before you leave? It would mean a lot to have this from you."

Once you receive the letter, you may also ask the person if he or she would be agreeable to serving as a verbal reference as well in the event that prospective employers want to know more about your work together.

Be aware of the timing of your reference requests. Don't ask someone who is mad at you or someone who knows you're in hot water with management. It puts this person on the spot unfairly and won't reflect well on you. Similarly, do not approach someone who doesn't know you well enough to have formed an opinion about your work. Ask someone who knows you and your work ethic and has some experience working with you.

ASK FOR CHARACTER REFERENCES. If you have been out of the workplace for a while, but have cultivated an impressive personal network, use those contacts. The fact that you didn't get paid for your work doesn't mean it wasn't valuable. For example, perhaps you served on the PTA at your children's school, where you've been instrumental in fund-raising. Ask the principal to write a reference letter that speaks about your character and tireless devotion to the causes and committees you served. Similarly, if there's a charitable organization for which you've planned and executed numerous events, you should ask the head of the group and even the honorary chairperson, especially if it's someone well-known, to write letters about your contributions. In some cases, you may have done your volunteer work alongside people who hold impressive positions. Ask them to write letters for you that address their professional qualifications for judging your abilities. For example, the cochair of your charity event might be the senior vice president of a local bank. He should identify his volunteer role and his professional position in the letter of reference; doing so will give it more clout. Other options: the leader of your religious congregation, former professors, and former part-time employers.

REFERENCE CHECKS. Interview your references before you add them to your list. Ask them what they would say about you. You must be satisfied with the answers and information they would provide if asked basic or thorough questions by any potential employer. Common questions your references may be asked include:

- Can you tell me about your relationship with her?

- What were her responsibilities, and did she fulfill them?

- Would you hire her for a full-time role or rehire her if you had the chance?

- How does she work with others, and would you share an example?

- Can you tell me about a mistake she has made and how she dealt with it?

- Can you tell me about her weaknesses or the areas in which she needs to develop?

Remember that the role of a reference is to seal the deal, not nix the offer. Do not request references or use names of people if you aren't completely certain of what they'll say about you and your character. If in doubt, leave them out.

How to Ask for Help from an Unknown College Alumnus

College alumni are an often-untapped resource, which is a shame since they can be some of your best connections for career networking. Begin asking for assistance with the right attitude.

ASK FOR NAMES. Contact your college's career-services office, its alumni-relations group, or its local alumni club to inquire about former students, e-mail addresses, employer names, and job titles for the people you wish to reach. Don't limit yourself to alumni working in professions you are interested in; focus on specific companies as well.

ASK FOR ADVICE. Instead of asking for a job, start by offering alumni the opportunity to share their career advice and individual stories. Alumni are usually eager to share career moves as well as to discuss current trends inside their organizations and within their industries as a whole.

DO YOUR HOMEWORK. Before contacting an alumnus, research his or her company. Familiarize yourself with the organization's structure, products and services, and competitors, as well as how this person's job fits into the organization.

Create a list of questions to ask based on your individual goals and the knowledge you have gained through your research. Among the potential questions:

- Why does this type of work interest you, and how did you get started?

- What do you find most satisfying in your work?

- What are the major frustrations in your job?

- If you had to start over, would you pick this role again? What about this company?

- What are the top skills someone must possess to be successful in this line of work?

- What advice would you give to someone starting out in or looking to break into this field?

- What professional organizations do you consider most beneficial for career development?

- What is the current hiring outlook for your organization? How does that differ from the hiring outlook in the industry as a whole?

SEND AN INTRODUCTORY E-MAIL. Indicate on the subject line who referred you. The first sentence should explain the context of your connection to that person. Next, provide a very brief summary of your current job status. Be specific about why you selected this particular person for advice and what information you are hoping to gain from a conversation or meeting. Ask to schedule a convenient time to call or meet for an informational interview for career information and advice. "Since I'm looking to break into the pharmaceutical-sales industry after 10 years in technology sales, I know you would be able to share valuable information with me about your time at Pfizer. Would you be agreeable to scheduling a time to talk by phone or in person?"

MAKE A PLAN. Once you develop rapport, it's okay to ask directly for contacts from whom you might obtain information and advice. Other acceptable questions include:

- Would you be willing to review my résumé and provide feedback?

- Do you have any advice on specific steps I should take to advance my career?

- Do you know of any current employment opportunities that would be right for me?

OFFER TO RECIPROCATE. Allow alumni the chance to ask questions about current life on campus since this can trigger a fun sense of nostalgia. It is also an opportunity for them to know who's recruiting on campus and what kind of career opportunities new graduates are currently pursuing. If you're an experienced professional and your own career comes up as a subject during the conversation, share information about it.

EXPRESS YOUR APPRECIATION. Send a thank-you note within 24 hours of your first conversation. If there's the potential of keeping in touch, be sure to say, "I will keep you posted on my progress. I hope you won't mind my asking additional questions if I have any in the near future."

FOLLOW THROUGH. Take action and follow through on all suggestions offered by alumni. Keep in contact and offer updates on how their advice has helped you.

REGISTER FOR UPDATES. Many universities provide structured programs and resources to help students and alumni connect with alumni who have similar careers. Contact your career-services center and ask about programs that provide access to your alumni network.

RECIPROCITY AGREEMENTS. If you attended a small college and you've found that none of the alumni connections are of value to your career, you should ask the current alumni or career-services director to assist you in establishing a reciprocity agreement with another college or university in your new location that you believe would be more helpful. Such arrangements allow you to tap into that network and make use of their resources, in exchange for your alma mater's offering the same to other alumni in need.

Contributor: Susan Filkins, coordinator, Alumni Programs, Center for Career Services at Syracuse University

How to Ask for a Lunch Date

Let's have lunch is a phrase often used meaninglessly. In business, avoid extending an invitation to lunch unless you are fully prepared

She Should Ask for It!

Catherine Zeta-Jones and Warner Brothers bought the film rights to my book *The Ivy Chronicles*. I wanted to ask Catherine to appear with me at a reading from the paperback edition. But I didn't ask because I decided that, since she's such a big star and has so many professional and family obligations, she would never say yes. I rejected the proposition for her before she had a chance to consider it. Now I realize that if I ask and she says no, I'll be in exactly the same position I am in now. Come to think about it, I may go ahead and ask her.

—KAREN QUINN, author, *The Ivy Chronicles* and *Wife in the Fast Lane*

to follow up. We all know that really big business occurs over lunch and even breakfast. How you make the invitation often determines whether or not you'll achieve the response and results you desire.

WHOM TO ASK. If you work on high-volume accounts, consider taking your clients to lunch every so often. Seize upon opportunities to show your appreciation for their business and to grow the professional relationship so that you'll be able to serve them even better. If a great project is nearing completion and you're looking to extend the contract, say, "After the end of this project, I would love to take you to lunch. It's been such a pleasure working with you, and I'd welcome the chance to discuss other ways we might support you." If there are prospective clients whom you're trying to lure, the lunch setting provides an easy way to get to know them and to increase your chances of landing their business. In such a case you might say, "I'm interested in learning more about your needs since my company might be able to offer some expertise to advance your cause. Would you be agreeable to having lunch to discuss this?"

Generally you should avoid inviting your superiors to lunch. It's awkward, and you're likely to be shot down, especially since most of the issues you would want to discuss with senior management should be brought up during a formal meeting. However, you're entitled— and highly encouraged—to invite colleagues to lunch. Sharing meals is a great way to grow relationships and build camaraderie within your own department and to get to know people in other departments.

Whether or not you are currently employed, use lunches as a way to get better acquainted with peers in your industry. These tasty meetings can do more than just expand your waistline; they can also broaden your knowledge and understanding of others who've been in your shoes.

When you do ask someone to lunch, be clear in stating the reason you want to meet. Sometimes, you simply want to catch up. Other times, you want to initiate business. Or you may want to pitch her or him a great idea. Maybe you want career advice. All of these are perfectly acceptable reasons. If you're doing the asking, say, "I want to take you to lunch as my guest." Sometimes knowing that there are no financial strings attached will free the other person up to accept your invitation.

If you have budget concerns, a less-expensive alternative to lunch is meeting for coffee, either at midmorning or at midafternoon. Anyone who has been to a Starbucks midday knows there are plenty of professional dialogues taking place. This arrangement also accommodates tighter schedules that preclude lunch.

ETIQUETTE. Make a reservation at a place that is convenient for you and your guest and that can accommodate any special dietary restrictions she or he might have. To ensure that you get it right, you might ask at the time of receiving an acceptance to your invitation: "Do you have any special requests about the type of food or the location that would be best for you?" You might learn that anything and anyplace are fine. Or you will be told that the person doesn't like spicy food or is allergic to seafood. Once you've confirmed a time and place, give your guest those details, along with the name in which you've made the reservation and the phone number of the establishment.

On the day of your lunch, get to the restaurant early and let the server know you will be picking up the check. This is also an ideal time to meet the maître d' and insure that he knows you by name. Turn off your cell phone once the other party arrives, but no earlier in case the guest tries to reach you. Stand to greet your guest with a handshake and address him or her by name. "Thank you so much for taking the time to get together today, Catherine. It's so great to see you." If you are meeting a group of people, try to acknowledge them in order of rank. After you sit down, place your napkin in your lap. Start the conversation by focusing on the guest and his or her interests. When the moment is right, bring up your desire to work together or the other business issues on your agenda. Never press a guest for an on-the-spot decision unless he or she is comfortable offering one.

If you have to leave the table during lunch, place your napkin on the left side of your plate to indicate you are not yet finished. When you are finished eating, place your knife and fork horizontally across the plate. Take care of the bill once it is placed on the table. You will appear unprofessional if you yield to your guest's request to split the cost, especially if you've invited him or her. Follow up the lunch with a thank-you note and any next steps that might have been discussed.

If you promised to share a contact or pass along an article you had read, be sure to do so within 24 hours after the lunch. If your guest offered a contact or other material, wait 24 hours to see if the information is forthcoming. If it is not forthcoming within that time, you may call or e-mail him or her with a gentle reminder.

How to Ask for a Mentor

In order to advance in business, it is important to have a mentor, but many women lack this key to success. That's no surprise: with men still filling the majority of the top leadership positions at Fortune 500 companies, and with the time pressures many working women confront, finding a mentor may seem next to impossible to many women.

A good mentor can be a man or a woman, someone from a background similar or different from your own, or even your boss. The most important factor is that you and your mentor can comfortably exchange feedback and ideas. In any case, don't wait around for mentors to come to you—be proactive in finding one yourself.

DEFINE YOUR GOALS. The first step in finding a mentor is deciding exactly what kind of coaching and advice you are in need of. Begin by asking yourself the following questions. Then, write a list of the goals you are looking to accomplish.

She Asked for It!

I was so nervous! How could I get Peggy Klaus, successful author and much-in-demand Fortune 500 executive-communication coach, to take my call? After all, I was unknown, with just a small start-up business, while she had been featured and quoted extensively in a wide range of media.

After days of telling myself not to try to contact her, I decided it was now or never, so I went to her Web site and sent a message about my professional background, my admiration for her work, and my desire to work with her.

Within 30 minutes, her business manager called to set up a meeting! What was it about the way I asked that got an immediate response?

- People evaluate requests through the filter of WII-FM (What's in it for me?). I told Peggy what was in it for her (promotion for her book through my programs).

- People want to be spoken to in their own language and within their own frame of reference. I established my credibility by using references that were meaningful to her (my affiliations with Fortune 500 companies).

- People want to know that they made a difference in your life. I made it clear that Peggy's work had been useful to me.

—LYNNE FAIR HOMRICH, founder and president, Excellent Women, LLC

- Do you need advice on how to move to the next level?

- Do you need advice on how to manage your support staff?

- Do you need help in writing a report, press release, or presentation?

- Do you need the scoop on politics within the organization?

- Do you want insight on how to break into a new field?

MAKE A LIST OF POTENTIAL MENTORS. Match your needs with the people who might best be able to address them. You will want people who can assess your performance—people in the loop who believe in you and will help you find opportunities. Keep in mind that no one person can help you address all of these needs. Instead of searching for the perfect mentor, strive to become the mentee of several talented people. Begin by thinking about people at your organization who can address some of your issues and concerns, then make a list of all of these people. Think about who has the knowledge, background, experience, and influence to be able to help you move ahead. Keep in mind the following:

Who's had the experience you're seeking and knows the path required?

Who has the skills you want to acquire?

Who's the best manager?

Who's the most effective at meetings?

Who has his or her ear to the ground?

Consider individuals who might introduce you to a friend or colleague of theirs with a recommendation that they mentor you. People are often willing to guide someone if she is a friend of a friend of someone they know.

LOOK INSIDE AND OUTSIDE YOUR COMPANY. First determine if your company has a formal mentoring program within the organization. If it's not possible to find a mentor internally, look outside the company. Consider everyone in your network—relatives, friends, former bosses, coworkers, even professors. Consider professionals ranging from service providers to neighbors. Ask yourself, *Whom do I admire and respect? Who has already been a role model for me?* Consider joining a mentoring organization or checking out industry associations or alumni groups.

DO YOUR RESEARCH. Once you've compiled your list of possible mentors, make yourself visible to your top candidates and do some investigating. Find out what you can about each person's career trajectory. Know where he or she has worked and what he or she has accomplished, so that you know the right questions to ask. Talk to people who have worked with the person. Use the internet, company newsletters, or other library resources to find out more. Volunteer for projects that potential mentors work on so that you can showcase your talents. Also, try to find out what organizations that person works for outside of her or his regular job, and join those groups if you can. Do good work in these other arenas so that he or she can see you in action.

MAKE A CONNECTION. At an office or social event, approach your potential mentor. If this opportunity doesn't come along, then take it upon yourself to arrange a meeting. Even dropping by or placing a call to the person's office at the right moment can work in your favor. Keep your eyes open for his or her comings and goings; you just might find an opening.

When face-to-face with the person, ask a question. Women who've had great mentors suggest asking for advice about something related to your career or your work, especially something that might be linked to your potential mentor's career. Most people are flattered to be asked for advice. Be sure to prepare the questions beforehand and to take notes so that you can refer to the responses at a later date.

START SMALL. Don't scare off a potential mentor by asking for too much. The person may turn you down if the job seems too big or too time-consuming, so don't lay it all on your potential mentor at the get-go. Let the relationship evolve. Be realistic about what someone can give you and build your rapport over time. At first, leave the word *mentor* out of the conversation. You may want to end your first meeting by asking if the person would be willing to meet with you again to follow up on what you've discussed thus far.

Base your approach to a potential mentor on what you know about him or her and on the kind of relationship you have. Use your judgment. If you work with this person, you know his or her schedule and how much time he or she has available. If you don't, you might want to develop a phone or e-mail relationship or one that includes these means of communication. Of course, face-to-face contact creates the closest mentoring relationships, but compromise where necessary in order to get the mentor you want. Either way, let your mentor know how you'd like the relationship to work and the frequency of contact that you are hoping for. If the person turns you down, don't take it personally. He or she may just be too busy, so you should simply thank him or her and continue to look for other mentors. Be sure to keep that person in your network, though; you never know when he or she will have more time or can help in some other way.

GIVE BACK. A mentor usually has a goal in taking you on, and there's nothing wrong with that. When starting out, don't give your mentor the impression that you're in the relationship only to benefit yourself. Let him or her know of your respect and support and show that you are going to be helpful in return. Be loyal. Return kindness. Be your mentor's "press agent," and offer information you pick up in circles that he or she doesn't run in. Don't underestimate the value that you too can bring to the relationship.

Let the mentor know over time how much you appreciate his or her support. Mentors are delighted to hear that they made a difference, so stay in touch.

Continue following these steps in order to build your own board of directors, and keep in mind that smart individuals focus on their network in order to raise their net worth in the workplace.

Contributor: Catalyst, the leading research and advisory organization on women in business

She Should've Asked for It!

My biggest regret is not asking some of my mentors for more feedback. I always thought I was bothering them, but looking back. I know it would have been a great help to me, and they probably would have loved to do it.

—TIFFANY COCHRAN, television news anchor

How to Ask for a Business Card

A good rule of thumb when asking for a business card is to state a reason for the request. This is true even when asking for a card from a peer. You can say, "It was so great talking with you. Why don't we exchange cards and connect again at some point soon?" You can even initiate the exchange by handing over your business card first and then saying, "It was so great talking with you." Expect the other person to do the same. Some tried-and-true tips for the big exchange:

- Accept every card that you are given.

- Be selective when handing out your card.

- Refill your card case before any major event.

- Don't cross through old information with a pen.

- Only give out clean cards with current information.

- After an event, note on the card(s) you received where you met the person and specifics about the conversation.

When someone hands you a card, show respect by taking a moment to read it. Look at the person's title. Don't file that card in the place where you file your own. If you do, you risk giving out valuable contact information by mistake and appearing unprofessional and disorganized. Instead, place it in a spot in your pocket or purse designated for other people's cards.

WHEN TO ASK. A good time to ask for a card is at the end of a conversation. At this stage, you have established a connection. In many cases, you can be very direct. "I would really appreciate your business card, so that I can send you some information that I think you'd find valuable." Or, "I would love to have your card, so that I can thank you formally for your gracious advice."

Change tactics slightly when someone has more status than you. A good rule of thumb in this situation is to ask for the card indirectly. For example, you may be at a networking event where you have been introduced to the decision maker at a company you really want to work for. You talk for a little while and discover his division needs someone with your skills. You can say, "I'd love to follow up with you. Would you tell me the best way to reach you?" In this case, he will often hand you his card. He may direct you to speak with his assistant.

FOLLOW PROFESSIONAL ETIQUETTE. It's generally inappropriate to ask directly for a card when someone significantly outranks you. However, in those rare instances when the timing seems right, and you want to take the risk, soften the request by saying that you will treat the information respectfully. Be clear that you will not share the contact information with others, nor will you bombard the contact with calls and e-mails. Don't be disappointed if the person tells you he has no cards on him or if you're flat out rejected.

In some cases, you may find yourself speaking with someone whose contact information is as good as gold. He or she may be leading industry trends and in big demand. Never ask for a business card, but do ask for the appropriate contact information. For example, "It's been an honor to speak with you. The keynote speech you gave at the conference today was just superb. I work in university relations and would love to have you deliver an address at my school this spring. Whom may I approach about this?"

Quite often, this person will be on hand. You can then say, "I was just speaking with your company's CEO. I mentioned that we would love to have him deliver the keynote address at my university this spring. He directed me to speak with you. May I have your card, so that I can follow up with you next week?" Follow the same line of thought that you would use when asking for a card from anyone: show that a connection has been established and give the reason for the request.

How to Ask for a Referral to Another Contact

Oftentimes you know someone who knows someone who could help you achieve your career goals. You want to get to that third party quickly and efficiently. There are key ways to phrase your referral request in order to make this happen. Just as your primary-care physician makes referrals for specialists, your core group of friends, family, and colleagues can make referrals for you. But you must ask in the right way in order to overcome any reservations:

- Be very clear and up-front about what you want.

- Discuss what you intend to share, say, or propose.

- Indicate that you will not disseminate the contact information.

- State that you have something of benefit to offer this other person.

She Asked for It!

I have always been great at pitching and promoting others, but when it came to asking for anything for myself, I struggled.

One of my favorite experiences occurred in 1998 when I was interviewing the legendary singer Frankie Laine on my brand-new radio show, Starstyle®-Be the Star You Are! We were discussing his memorable song from the TV show *Rawhide,* and he mentioned that at one point in his career he was known as "the king of theme songs" because so many movies and TV shows showcased his songs.

With enthusiasm I blurted, "Frankie, we need an original song for this radio program. How about creating one for us?" The next day his producer called me to say that Frankié had so enjoyed the interview and my genuine passion for empowering others that he was gifting me with a theme song. Within a month, our station was playing our very own theme song, which is still the foundation for our program today.

What I learned is that when we ask for assistance, we give others an opportunity to be of service. Most successful people enjoy helping others become successful. It is part of their gift to the world.

—CYNTHIA BRIAN, coauthor, *Chicken Soup for the Gardener's Soul,*
and radio show host

DO YOUR HOMEWORK. Know specifically why you want to contact this person. When phrasing a referral request, keep your focus on the benefit to the *other* person. For example, say, "I'd like to contact this individual because I know his division is looking for a graphic designer and I believe I'm one of the best. Could I give him a call?" Convey a sense of what's in it for the person you wish to contact. Then establish the next steps: Will you initiate contact? Or will the referring party make the initial call? Will you mention the referring party by name? Follow these strategies to increase the odds that the other party will respond positively:

ESTABLISH A CONNECTION. When you do make contact with the third party, try to establish a connection. If you just saw your mutual friend last week, mention that. If your friend spoke highly of this person, note that while trying to initiate a dialogue. For example, "I just saw Mike, and he mentioned you both went skiing last month. He said you two had a great time. You apparently were excellent on the slopes. Have you seen his photos of the trip yet?"

STATE WHY YOU ARE CALLING. Once you have established a connection, let this person know why you are calling. As you did with the referring party, focus on how you and your skills can benefit them. For example, say, "I know you are passionate about animal rights, and I am an animal-rights activist as well. My organization has a new initiative that I would love to discuss with you. Do you have a few moments?" Stay focused on maintaining a dialogue.

GUARANTEE FUTURE REFERRALS. Of course, remember to thank this person and the referring party as well. The more that you invest in your network, the easier it will be to ask for more referrals.

Think of each important relationship as a checking account: you need to match the deposits with the withdrawals; otherwise, you will become overdrawn. Send handwritten thank-you notes. Invest in small gifts. Also look for opportunities to return favors since remembering the right person at the right time creates an enduring bond of respect. Guard your time, but also know that to receive you must give. If someone contacts you asking for information or a referral, try to help her. Your goodness will come back to you. Pay it forward.

CLIENT REFERRALS. If, as a freelancer or independent consultant, you find yourself working for a corporation on a contract basis, it is appropriate to ask for referrals at the end of a project. Corporations have myriad departments likely to have a need for your services. Finish the project, send an invoice, confirm that the client is happy with your work, and send a thank-you note. You can say, "It was my pleasure working on this project. Are there any other divisions in your company in need of similar work? Is there someone else you could suggest that I contact?"

Develop a strategy for staying in touch with existing clients so that they will continue to refer you to friends and colleagues. Make them a part of your network. Send cards during the holidays and find a few more occasions to stay in touch year-round:

- Are you or your client featured in the press regularly? Can you intermittently send along press clippings with short notes?

- Can you speak at an industry event and send invitations to your key contacts?

- Can you conduct a study in your industry and share the results with your clients?

- Can you contribute to a trade magazine and share the published story with industry contacts?

Trade publications might allow you to write articles for them and are considered by industry leaders as prestigious vehicles for communicating the latest information. They can often help position you as a leader and might be more willing to do so than mainstream media. They could be a tremendous source of new referrals for you.

She Asked for It!

I am often asked to introduce someone else to a well-known or famous colleague that I am seen with on television or radio or know well personally. It's often extremely difficult for me to tap into those contacts since these people are not available to me on a regular basis and are inundated with calls and requests. The most important thing I must consider is if there would be a true benefit for both parties. I must feel as if I am performing a good deed for both people by making the introduction, since I take into serious consideration the privacy and needs of both. So many people ask friends of friends for help, but when doing so, you'll have a better shot if you present the clear value for the other party when making your request. And then when someone does introduce you to someone new, write a note of thanks or call and let her know that she made a valuable introduction.

—ROBYN SPIZMAN, author, television and radio personality

How to Ask for a Second Chance to Make a Good Impression

In business, we have finite time to make a lasting impression on decision makers. A myriad of factors must work in your favor on the day of a meeting. Only some of them are within your control. Sometimes, despite the best of intentions, you'll fail to make an impression. You didn't put your best foot forward. You said the wrong thing. You were late. You were feeling under the weather. You blew it!

In this case, you have a few options. You can brush it off. You can convince yourself that no one noticed. Or you can be proactive and try to make it better. You can ask for forgiveness and a second chance.

First step: apologize. Offer a brief explanation. Acknowledge what you did wrong. Then ask for a second meeting. "I'm so sorry I didn't have the materials prepared for our meeting yesterday. This meeting was very important to me, and I would love the chance to speak with you again. Do you have any time next week?" Another option is to say, "I apologize for being unprepared yesterday. I inadvertently forgot the materials, but I'd be happy to send them to you now to peruse. Would you mind giving me 15 minutes next week to review them with you in person?"

In cases in which you have trouble reaching the other person by phone, consider leaving a voice mail or sending an e-mail. You can clearly explain what went wrong—again, brevity is a must—and what you would like to do going forward. Handle this message as you would if you had that person live on the line. Do not beat up on yourself or refer to yourself as an idiot or moron—a mistake many women make. Close by suggesting days and times when you will be available. "I would really like to meet with you again. Would you have any time next Wednesday or Thursday?"

If you know for sure that you fumbled through several interview questions or were stumped by some of them, replay the conversation in your mind and share the details with a trusted friend to determine if it was really as bad as you imagined it to be. Sometimes we're too hard on ourselves, and in reality the other party didn't notice anything awry. Before admitting that you goofed, be sure that you really did. In such a case, send a note or place a call saying, "I realize I wasn't myself yesterday. I don't have an excuse to offer you, but I'm hoping you'll consider meeting with me again because I'm expertly qualified for this position. I just need a second chance to make a better impression. Would you please consider this request?"

Another way to compensate for messing up the first time is to focus on the needs of the other person and how you're uniquely qualified to meet them. Suggest a solution to a problem that was discussed during the initial meeting; this solution should demonstrate your added value. Draw on past work experience and give examples of your successes. "Despite arriving late for the meeting, for which I apologize, I know I would be an excellent fit with your company. You mentioned initially that you are trying to cut costs. I have been able to reduce costs by 20 percent in my division over the past four years. I have some solutions I would love to discuss with you."

You don't want to make a negative impression before you even arrive. If you know you'll be late to an interview or meeting, don't keep staring at the clock hoping that you'll somehow make it in the nick of time. Instead, call in advance and notify someone of your delay. Provide a realistic time frame in which you expect to arrive, and be sure it is ample. "I'm so sorry about this, but I'm stuck in traffic, which means I won't be there for about 20 minutes. I hope a half hour delay won't inconvenience you too much. I have all the materials for a terrific presentation, so I promise it'll be worth this unexpected wait."

If you didn't put your best foot forward the first time—maybe your presentation was weak, or you came across as moody—focus on establishing your professional value after the fact. For example, were you recently featured in the press? Send the news clipping. Did you recently receive a prestigious award? Has your work been cited for excellence? Send a copy of the honor with a positive note sharing your excitement about the award, but avoid boasting. Your continued good work will speak for itself. Do you have a Web site that highlights your professional accomplishments? Send the link. Don't expect immediate feedback, but know that you are developing rapport and working to polish an image that might have been slightly tarnished.

How to Ask for an Invitation to a High-Profile Event

By attending high-profile events, you can further both your professional development and your business development. Ask to attend from one of these two perspectives, and always approach the events strategically.

PROFESSIONAL DEVELOPMENT. Your attendance at high-profile events is an investment for you and your company. When you ask to attend, you might say, "I know that every year the executive team meets in London during Wimbledon. Given the responsibilities that I currently have at this company, I think it would be very beneficial for me to attend. I am on the phone with these people all the time. I notice that when I am more visible, they are much more receptive to my calls and recognize the contribution that I am mak-

She Asked for It!

I got some good advice from a mentor early in my career. I was told, "No one is sitting around above you wondering how he can make your professional experience better, how he can help you with your career, and how he can make your job more satisfying."

Her advice was that, when you feel you've hit a point in the road at which you need to expand, to change, or to take on new responsibilities, you really have to ask your boss for what you want. Ask with the answers and possible solutions in mind. Many times the person you are working for has a host of other responsibilities, and if you really want him to take you seriously, then you have to make it as easy as possible for him to do so.

—SUSAN HOOK, senior director of Corporate Communications, Red Envelope

ing to the team. This year, I would like to go over for a few days. Would this be possible?"

You may hear: "Let me think about it." Ask for a time frame in which you should follow up. Then do so. If you sense any hesitation, you can say, "If cost is an issue, I don't need to be there for the whole week. However, I'd like to be able to monitor the executive session. Please let me know your thoughts."

Perhaps you have worked tirelessly on the planning and execution of your company's annual shareholders' meeting. The work is nearing completion, and the big day is drawing near. Your boss will be attending, but there's been no mention of inviting you. You may say, "I realize this event does not cater to employees at my level.

However, since I've been intimately involved with every detail, it would mean a lot to me to attend. I view this as important to my professional development since it would benefit my work on future events. Would you consider including me?"

BUSINESS DEVELOPMENT. Alternatively, you might want to attend for business-development reasons. In this situation, you might say, "Attending the meeting in London next month is important. Our biggest client is going to be there. I deal with them on the phone constantly. I'm the one filing the reports, and I'm the one doing their numbers. I know they are very pleased with and excited by our work. I think that if I was there, I would be able to help the team close additional business."

Another example is the kind of industry-specific function that is typically reserved for the senior executives of related companies. If you can identify a business need, you stand a better chance of securing a ticket. Your company might be trying to do business with leaders in the fashion industry. You know that the annual costume ball at the Metropolitan Museum of Art in New York is a veritable Who's Who of that world. Tickets are $2,500 per person, but if you make even one strong connection, it will have been worth it.

KNOW THE AGENDA. Before you attend a high-profile event, do your research. Know a little about the backdrop event for the meeting. If this is Wimbledon, know the key players and how they have done during the season. If someone has staged a comeback, make sure you know the details. Be able to talk about it. Likewise, familiarize yourself with the key players for the main function, which is the corporate event. Understand why they get together at the backdrop event. Know the underlying agenda. If you can add value to that agenda, you can more easily build a case for being there. Understand that backdrop events always revolve around business concerns, no matter how exciting or high-profile these backdrop events may be.

AD"DRESS" THE DETAILS. How you present yourself at these events is critically important. Don't arrive looking disheveled and complaining about jet lag and the crummy room service back at the hotel. Although this may be fodder for bonding with your friends socially, it won't work professionally.

When you participate in important functions, you should look the part: If you are attending a high-profile event at a polo field, consider wearing a hat and a fancy sundress. If you are attending one at a tennis match, consider wearing white. If it's a formal business dinner, you'll want a very fine suit and appropriately elegant accessories. This is a time when you want to give a lot of consideration to what is the norm and to dovetailing it with some creative flair. Little details in your self-presentation—from whether or not your shoes are shined to how low your sleeves and hem are—speak volumes about you and your professionalism.

Many people regard these events as the highlights of their careers; others see them as a nuisance that goes with the territory. Focus on having some good times and doing some concentrated networking. Have fun, but remember why you are there.

How to Ask About Sports
When You Know Very Little About the Topic

The fact that sports has its own daily section in every major newspaper—unlike travel, fashion, automobiles, and other popular subjects—tells you something about its significance in our society. This popularity and prominence make sports an ideal icebreaker in many business settings, especially when peers are unaware of any other common ground.

Most businessmen follow some aspect of sports closely, and they're passionate about it. As a woman in business you don't have to follow every score, player, or stat, nor do sports have to be your cup of tea, but you're likely to be perceived as out of the loop if you don't know who won the World Series or the Super Bowl. The benefits extend far beyond being on the same playing field as men. Women today are actively engaged in sports on all levels and have found a tremendous amount of satisfaction from the spectator's side as well as that of the participants, especially in golf, tennis, cycling, and skiing. Becoming interested in sports is exciting and invigorating. Plus, learning about sports allows you the opportunity to understand a variety of games, businesses, and passions. It connects you to people's interests while also helping you to develop new hobbies and interests of your own.

Jump-start your own game plan by developing a baseline level of sports knowledge so that you can talk the talk and get started. If a new colleague says he's from Massachusetts, you can hit it off with him by asking if he's a Red Sox fan. Similarly, if your local team is in the NBA play-offs, there's no excuse not to be able to share in this excitement.

To ace the essentials of asking about a peer's or a colleague's interest in sports without getting bogged down in details, concentrate on a twofold focus that includes both local teams and national events:

- GET TO KNOW YOUR HOME TURF. Make a habit of reading the headlines in the sports pages every day or tuning in to the sports segment of your local television or radio news to learn how your local teams are performing. Be able to name the football, basketball, and hockey teams in your area in case you're asked about them. In addition to knowing the star players, as a businessperson you'll want to pay particular attention to leadership challenges or changes in team ownership and coaching staffs.

- PAY ATTENTION TO THE BIG LEAGUES. There is a handful of world and national sporting events that capture the headlines and the interest of our country. Among the most important to follow: the Super Bowl, the World Series, the NBA finals, the U.S. Open, Wimbledon, the Masters, the Stanley Cup, and the Kentucky Derby. Focus on top performers and any ensuing controversial calls.

While familiarity with these events requires dedicated effort, the payoff can be enormous in terms of forging meaningful business relationships. Knowledge of sports gives you plenty of ways to grease the conversational wheels, and you'll earn the respect of new colleagues, especially the men, when you ask about their favorite teams. You'll also feel better connected to individuals who are complete sports fanatics. And the sporting world just might gain a brand-new fan when you discover that it can actually be fun and enjoyable.

Office Etiquette

How to Cancel a Prior Commitment or Appointment

Sometimes we make appointments that we can't keep. Other times we don't want to honor our appointments, and we need a gracious way out. Consider the importance of the agenda and the people involved and then decide the appropriate course of action. Take care in making your decisions since you don't want to burn any bridges.

POSTPONING. For important meetings, always ask about postponing. For example, ask, "How would you feel about moving this meeting to next week?" This technique allows you to explore the possibility of rescheduling. In some cases, you will discover you cannot. For example, the person you need to meet with may be traveling over the next several weeks. When you know that you cannot reschedule a meeting, you have the opportunity to evaluate your conflicting appointments and to set priorities.

When you ask someone to postpone a meeting, you show respect by involving that person in the decision. Say, "Would you mind if we postponed our meeting?" Almost invariably, this person will say, "No problem," and agree to a new date. Apologize and offer a brief explanation. Say, "I'm really sorry. I found myself in the midst of deadlines."

CANCELING. There will be times, however, when you definitely want to cancel. You agreed to meet with someone and wish you hadn't, because the meeting isn't a smart use of your time, or you realize that you can't be of much help. In any of these cases, tell the person why you are canceling. Say, "I'm sorry for any inconvenience, but I'm going to have to cancel our appointment. I'm very busy, and I can't fit this into my schedule. I may be able to suggest a better person for you to meet with based on your needs." Try to give a nugget of direction or advice. But be firm about your inability to honor this commitment.

Avoid giving an excuse that's not true. For example, don't say that you have a doctor's appointment or that a more urgent meeting just came up. This suggests that you would like to reschedule, when you really want to cancel. Take care of it decisively by being direct and canceling without an excuse. For example, "I apologize for the short notice, but I am not able to fit this into my schedule."

ETIQUETTE FOR POSTPONING AND CANCELING. Postponing and canceling meetings may be done by phone or by e-mail. Plan your strategy. Last-minute cancellations should be done by phone to ensure that your message has been received. Postponements may be done by e-mail, but consider the other person's responsiveness. When he or she is less responsive or is someone you don't know well, or when the meeting is really critical, a personal call with your regrets is always best. You don't want the person to expunge you from his schedule before you have a chance to talk to him. Leave your name and number with an assistant for a callback, but avoid voice mail.

The more senior you become in business, the more you will be dealing with this issue—even when you have a gatekeeper. You may agree to a meeting in a moment of weakness. Or something that seemed like a good idea a month ago may not seem like a good idea now. In these cases, you can easily cancel by e-mail. E-mail allows you to be direct and thoughtful without stumbling over your words. It also documents the fact that you have canceled, but make sure you get a response so that the individual isn't left waiting for you in a restaurant. Consider following up with the person by voice mail at the end of the day. Say, "I just wanted to follow up on my message to you today. I'm so sorry that I've had to cancel. This has been an un-usually busy time for me."

Successful businesspeople know how to manage their time, and they trust their instincts. Be as helpful as you can, but respect the fact that you are someone with limited time and resources. Prioritize your relationships and your commitments.

How to Ask for Help on a Project

Quite often, women don't ask for help at work, but are more than willing to have other people's work dumped on them. We women of-fer our assistance to colleagues in need, but when it comes to our-selves, we worry that we will be perceived as incompetent or needy if we ask for the same help. So, we just try to do it all on our own, which is a mistake.

Asking for help is about managing your time and your career.

She Asked for It!

I used to be worried that I was asking for too much and that my doing so would anger people. My husband, Brad, an investment banker, helped me realize that management usually has leeway in providing services. I learned to negotiate for Town Car rides and first-class travel. I never ask for more vacation, since I never get to take it.

I was horrified to have to take bed rest when I was pregnant with my twins—I'm the kind of woman who takes just a few weeks' maternity leave. But I was exhausted and needed the rest, and I made it a straightforward request. CNN was very happy to oblige.

I have accepted way too many events. Even with four small children, I always try to squeeze them all in. Finally, when my morning show went to four hours, I canceled all my events. Now I accept almost none. For the first time I am enjoying free afternoons and hanging out, instead of running frantically from event to event.

So one of the things of which I am most proud is achieving the ability to say no—to requests from work, from friends, from acquaintances. No, no, no.

You'd be amazed at how brazen and annoyed people can be when you turn them down. Unfortunately I need the excuse of getting up at 2:30 A.M. Getting up at 3:30 A.M. and having four kids wasn't enough!

—SOLEDAD O'BRIEN, anchor, CNN

Asking for help need not diminish your strengths or abilities in any way. In fact, there's a lot of grace in asking for assistance, and here's why:

- Perhaps there is a specific expertise that is required on a project, and you do not possess it.

- Maybe there is a deadline that you are in danger of missing unless you get some help.

- You might be juggling several priorities simultaneously, and you need an extra hand.

- You received a new responsibility at work but lack the necessary training.

By failing to ask for help, you may miss a deadline, which will no doubt reflect poorly on you. Don't hesitate to ask for help when you need it. Instead of risking failure, figure out what you need in order to produce a successful outcome, and try to communicate that need early in the process. By asking for more help, you may be eliminating potential problems.

The key is how you ask for that help. Don't approach your boss and say, "I'm so overwhelmed, I can't handle this." Instead say, "There is so much text in this presentation. I want to bring in a copywriter to make sure we deliver a flawless presentation." Keep the focus off yourself and on the benefit to the employer. You are players on the same team, and you are looking for a win. You've studied the issue and know how to ensure a win.

Handling your job this way demonstrates that you understand the critical aspects of the project and are willing to delegate some aspects of it that may be outside your core competency. Don't say, "I'm just not confident in my abilities as a copywriter." Instead, say, "We need a professional writer to really make this shine."

The next time you are working on a project that increases in scope so much that it becomes hard to handle, say, "We really need to pull two additional people into this project because it increased in scope since we received the assignment. I want to ensure we meet the agreed-upon deadline." Don't say, "I'm terrified that I'm going to miss a deadline so I really need more help." It's all in the way that you position the request. It's all in the way you ask.

Try to ask for help as soon as you see a problem. But even if trouble brews up at the eleventh hour, remember to ask for the appropriate assistance. There is minimal risk in asking for help, while there is great risk in not asking.

She Asked for It!

I don't have a difficult time asking my coworkers to assist me when I need extra help. I feel it's in the spirit of the workplace that we co-operate with and unconditionally help each other whenever possible. When I demonstrate an appreciation of the need for helping others, it's also much easier and more comfortable to ask for help.

It's not about giving so that you receive; it's about giving because it's the right thing to do. If I come in with a positive attitude, I can influence others around me and help open up communication for everyone, so that they can ask for what they need and support each other.

—GAIL HEYMAN, registered dental hygienist

How to Ask to Delegate a Responsibility

Learning to delegate is essential. To delegate, you must have a clear understanding of your responsibilities and the parameters of your job. When you ask your boss for permission to delegate, show the benefit to the company. Say, "I'm spending a lot of time handling the invoicing, which is taking away from my ability to effectively handle the sales calls. If we could have someone else handle the invoicing, I could devote more time to generating revenue."

Unless you are an administrative assistant or coordinator, consider delegating activities such as: data entry, fact-finding assignments, collecting data for reports, photocopying, printing and collating, scheduling appointments, and tasks outside your core competency that you don't want or need to gain skills in.

When you delegate a project, you must still take responsibility for its successful completion. However, you need to give your designee the freedom and authority to complete that task. Explain why the task is important, why you are delegating it, and what your expectations are.

You may want to frame your request to delegate from the perspective of trying to groom another person or training someone else as backup. For example, you can say to your boss, "I've recently discovered that it would probably make a lot more sense for Mary to handle this task. I think it would be great training for her. Since the company has a strong policy of promoting from within, it would be very beneficial for her to have this experience."

Expect to have some concerns at first. In order to delegate, you may have to overcome your lack of confidence in your subordinates. You may be a perfectionist and think that delegating will produce inferior work. It may also make you feel professionally insecure. You may feel territorial and apprehensive about the lack of control. These are common concerns, and you need to work through them.

- Delegating work can be a calculated risk.

- Learning to delegate and giving up control may be the toughest part of your job.

- Delegating provides your subordinate with new challenges.

- Delegating allows you to accomplish substantially more work.

- Successful delegating builds your reputation within the company.

If the task is something simple, you don't need to ask your boss for permission to delegate it. Simply ask a subordinate or coworker directly. Maybe this will mean going to an assistant and saying, "I was wondering if you would be willing to take this on. It will give you some really great experience." In some cases, you may want to phrase your request with a compliment: "You are such a smart and talented person. What would you think of handling this?" To ensure that everyone stays on track to complete a project:

- Ask for progress reports.

- Review a sampling of the work to make sure it's being done the way you want.

- Put interim deadlines in writing.

- Delegate to a variety of people if there are multiple tasks to be completed.

- Trust your subordinates and don't look over their shoulders.

- Be prepared to accept short-term errors in order to get long-term results.

- Specify the objective, but not the method for achieving it, though you may offer suggestions and feedback.

When you delegate successfully, you enable others to showcase their competence and gain confidence. You may also save your company money by having tasks completed by qualified employees and freeing yourself to do more value-added kinds of work.

How to Ask for More Training

People are often reluctant to ask for more training because they think that their doing so is a poor reflection on them. Be certain to avoid that fear because learning new skills is an excellent way to manage your career and to get ahead. Just be sure you position your request carefully and confidently. When you ask for training, say that it will enhance your ability to do your job. Be prepared, too, to show how this training will benefit the company. Whether you are asking for help from a colleague, requesting permission to partake in a company program, or writing a proposal asking for outside training, take pride in the fact that you want to be at the top of your game.

Ask about training as early as when you interview for a job. Most companies see it as a smart investment in their employees. Later on, you can also refer to what your benefits package says about the availability of internal programs and browse the intranet for this type of information. Here are the key steps:

- Ask around to see whether your company covers training expenses and what kinds of courses are included.

- Complete any standard paperwork issued by the employer.

- Research your options with respect to training and continuing education.

- Ask for suggestions from coworkers and your human-resources department.

- List your training choices, and include fees for any external programs on your list.

- Show how this training will improve your performance *and benefit the company*.

- Schedule time in which to present the information you have gathered to your manager or human-resources department.

- State why this is a good investment of time and money.

- Expect your boss to have to sign off on your request.

Before assuming you need training through formal course work, consider asking a colleague as the easier solution. Say you are being called upon to do an increasing number of PowerPoint presentations, and you're just not good at creating a clever slide show. Approach colleagues who are highly skilled at this program and compliment them on their technical abilities. Then suggest to them ways that you might be trained to do the same work. Ask, "Would you be willing to spend some time guiding me through your own tutorial on PowerPoint? Or is there a type of training that worked well for you and that you could suggest to me? I'd really appreciate any tips you might have because I could benefit from your expertise." You could also offer to do the research necessary to find the training if it's not readily available. Knowing how much it would cost and the time it would require away from the job could help you accomplish your goal.

This technique can also be used to problem-solve mundane tasks around the office, such as learning to fix a printer. Ask a colleague by saying, "Every time the printer breaks, you know how to get it up and running again. I feel bad that we always have to call on you. I was wondering if you could make some time to train me so that I can troubleshoot this problem myself?"

EXTERNAL TRAINING. Before you seek outside training, you will need to ask your boss for permission to do so. Present a couple of options and explain how they would benefit you and the company. Expect to follow up with a written proposal, which may be a detailed report or a simple one-sheet. It should reiterate why you need the training, where you can get it, the cost, and, most importantly, the benefit to the company. Avoid saying, "I can't do my job without this training." Instead say, "I could do my job even better with this training."

When your request is approved, learn the parameters. You may be restricted by what you can submit for reimbursement or when you can attend classes. Ask for this information in writing. Anticipate having to share your knowledge. Your boss may ask you to give a group presentation or to write an essay, so save your notes and all the course materials. Even if he doesn't ask you to share your information, volunteer to conduct a "lunch-and-learn" for your colleagues.

If your proposal is turned down, ask why. If funding is a concern, suggest less-expensive alternatives like taking an evening enrichment program or a night course at a community college, or ask to be placed on a waiting list for funds. If you didn't prove that this type of training would be valuable to the company, find out what would be of value to it. But if you feel you need the training to ensure your own personal success, take a night or weekend class and go for it. Regardless of the outcome, asking for more training shows a proactive approach to your career, so start asking as soon as you anticipate a need.

How to Ask to Hire an Assistant

Are you starting a new project? Have you been given a promotion? Has your workload become so overwhelming that you're trapped underneath a pile of still-to-be-done tasks? An assistant is what you need—short-term or long-term—but asking for one is a challenge for many women. You will need to be able to justify to your employer the extra pay that will go to another person for doing what is arguably your work. The key is showing the big benefits of bringing on that additional person.

SURE SIGNS. Among the reasons you should not shy away from insisting on additional resources are the following:

- Your boss recently added much more responsibility to your plate, and you need a temporary assistant in order to meet your deadlines.

- Your initial position was supposed to cover only so much ground, but because of company growth, staff turnover, or superiors' improper delegating, you are currently being asked to do more than is possible. A pay raise would make you feel appreciated, but the work would still be waiting to be tackled. You really need help so that you can get the work done and achieve the results expected.

JUSTIFY IT. Your employer—and you for that matter—need to be assured that asking for an assistant won't be misinterpreted as your falling down on the job or not being able to keep up with your work allotment. Instead, point out that you are asking for assistance with administrative or transactional tasks to free yourself up to focus on more value-added work. Meet face-to-face with your boss to explain item by item what you're facing and why you're seeking additional resources.

- List your daily tasks, and the time required to fill each one.

- Say where the deficits are and/or what the new project will be, so that you and your employer will have an organized overview of what needs to be accomplished.

- *Your assistant:* Ideally, should she be part-time or full-time, temporary or permanent?

- *Your assistant's tasks:* What would you initially want her to handle once her training was completed?

Describe to your employer how having an assistant will allow you to take on new projects and focus on revenue-producing activities. "There is no way I can do what I normally do and also accomplish the additional tasks recently assigned to me. We really need to talk about getting me some help. I've heard good things about the temp agency downtown, so I'd like to discuss bringing in someone to help me accomplish X, Y, and Z."

Another option: "I'm excited about the new accounts we've acquired. However, they more than triple my workload, and I haven't been given any new resources. I feel strongly that we must add an assistant to the team in order to get everything up and running with smooth efficiency."

STARTING OUT. Be sure to reveal at some point that results will not be immediate or automatic. You will need to hire the right person, assist her in developing the needed skills, and work with her to create trust. A good team takes time and effort to build, but with the foundation of strong potential and solid training, it will happen, and you'll both look good.

How to Ask a Colleague to Quit Complaining

In a work environment, there are different types of people with diverse personalities, all trying to work together. When it comes to complaining, the reasons and possibilities for doing so are endless. However, too much complaining commonly poses problems for others who are just trying to do their jobs. How do you recognize a chronic complainer, when do you step in, and how do you stop her?

She Asked for It!

I decided I wanted to become a judge. To do so, I had to run for the office and ask for people's votes. I had to ask for those votes every day throughout a very lengthy campaign. Initially, it was hard for me to promote myself, but I learned that sometimes you just have to put yourself out there and take a risk.

I decided the best way to go about it was to embrace who I am. I am not only a lawyer; I am a woman, a wife, and a mother. I focused not only on my legal experience, but also on my life experience. I explained to voters that the skills I had cultivated as a wife and mother enhanced my judgment and contributed to my ability to be a fair and impartial problem solver.

My focus on this life experience also enabled me to relate to the voters to whom I was speaking—a crucial factor in gaining their confidence. I found that by remaining genuine and true to myself, I was empowered to ask for people's votes, and that ultimately the act of asking for what I wanted became empowering in and of itself. The fact of the matter is that whatever we do in life, we are always asking for people's vote of confidence in us. I am glad that I took the risk and asked for the vote.

—THE HONORABLE JUDGE DEBRA BERNES, *The Court of Appeal of Georgia*

COMPLAINER PROFILES.

The "Good" Negative: This colleague is usually responsible and delivers strong results, but just has a negative attitude.

Solution: Initially it might be worthwhile to let her vent, but ultimately you must get to the bottom of her negativity. Approach her gently, without causing her to go on the defensive. "I sense that you've been very unhappy lately, and I'd like to discuss this. I know you often complain about answering to the other departments, which is understandable, especially since we can always count on you to get things done. Lately, though, your complaining has worried me. There must be some other issues going on, and I'm hoping you'll be willing to share them over lunch."

This approach will show your concern and help you uncover what is at the root of her complaints without hurting her feelings. Does she require more support in or feedback about her work? Is she experiencing a personal challenge outside of the office? Let her know that her negativity has the ability to bring everyone down and makes the work environment less livable.

The "Bad" Negative: This colleague allows her complaining to affect her work. She may even utilize it as a way to procrastinate and miss deadlines.

Solution: This type must be handled much like the previous one, except that the seriousness of her failure to perform must be emphasized.

"I need to understand why you're complaining all the time. Everyone has a bad day here and there, but your work is consistently incomplete, which is a poor reflection on our entire team. You may think you're the only one suffering, but you're actually bringing all of us down. Is there something I can do to help you to overcome any specific obstacles, or do you think it's better to bring this issue to our boss?"

The "Hopeless" Negative: This colleague doesn't really have a nasty attitude; she just seems helpless and hopeless—never happy with whatever solutions people come up with. It seems she complains just to complain. Regardless, you have grown weary of her complaining and need to put an end to it.

Solution: You may need to refer her to her boss.

"I feel I've done as much as I can. I've listened and offered a myriad of suggestions, all to no avail. You should talk to your supervisor since your behavior is affecting your work and mine. I'm sorry that it's come to this, but we both have work to accomplish."

STEP IN, STOP IT. There will be times when you will need to step in to try to help, and other times when you will need to laugh the complaining off—especially if the colleague is just venting. If you show that you will initially listen to and help guide the person, but beyond that you'll have little to no tolerance, then there is a good chance he or she will stop coming around you.

- Talk to your coworker early on. Don't let things bubble up, or else someone is likely to blow up.

- Don't allow yourself to be a victim of the three Bs: bickering, backstabbing, and blaming. When you get caught up with complainers, it's easy to fall victim to this nonsense.

Sometimes the causes of chronic complaining lie outside of work. Personal issues such as health, divorce, or finances require assistance that you, as a coworker, can't and shouldn't provide. If outside-of-work issues are affecting a colleague, refer her or him to the employee-assistance program, where trained professionals can help.

Another option is to discuss the problems with your manager and let him try to get to the root of the issue. It may be time for the complainer to transfer to a department that offers more challenges or just a change of pace. If the issues can't be resolved and the employee's performance does not improve, then termination may be the result. Since that step is likely beyond your authority, it's important to have involved the senior managers in the dilemma. Workers need to have a healthy atmosphere in the workplace. By showing you care, you've tried to make your own workplace healthier for yourself and others.

How to Ask a Coworker to Stop Wearing Strong Perfume

In the workplace, good grooming is not only an enhancement, it is a necessity. But what happens when it is carried too far—when something like a nice fresh scent turns into an overpowering smell that makes others nauseous and creates discord between coworkers?

OFFENSIVE OR SUBJECTIVE? With few exceptions, women who wear too much perfume do so because they want to be able to smell it themselves; in fact, they may become immune to the smell over time, and therefore they will spray more of the perfume. They will keep spritzing it until they can smell it at the right potency. By then, it's too much, and it can leave their office mates begging for air.

These coworkers—especially those more sensitive to smells—may experience allergy flare-ups, nausea, headaches, and even minor difficulties breathing. Sometimes you're too shy to say anything, and your hints—a fan, coughing, sneezing, gagging—fail to persuade the colleague to neutralize or minimize her scent.

SMELL SOLUTIONS.

- *Be honest.* If you have an allergy or are highly sensitive to smells and this is a major concern for you, share your problem in private and tell the colleague honestly that perfume can make you really ill. Ask if she would mind not wearing any since perfume can mean medical consequences for you. Tell her you would be very appreciative of the favor. Most individuals who are allergic to perfume are also sensitive to odors from many sources, ranging from oil-based paints to potent glues, so it's a good idea to make your allergies known to your coworkers whenever possible and in a positive way before something else happens and pulls the trigger on your allergies.

- *Cordial communication.* There's no reason to openly embarrass or criticize the coworker, so be courteous, tactful, and private when making your point. You can suggest she tone it down without actually asking her to. "The perfume that you wear is very unique. It's such a very rich scent, and you probably don't realize, but it's overpowering at times. I've done that myself with a favorite scent."

- *Offer a solution.* It's always better to follow up a complaint with a solution or suggestion. "The experts in the fashion magazines are always quoted as saying one spritz before you walk out the door in the morning is ideal. I've tried that, and it really works! You might want to try it tomorrow and see if you can tell the difference."

- *Remind her.* If she follows your advice for a while, but later on relaxes into her old habits, remind her. "Do you know that if you wear the same fragrance all the time, you become immune to the smell? That's probably why you're using too much perfume again."

- *Company policy.* If your coworker insists on ignoring you, go to human resources and ask about the policy for such situations. Some policies restrict overuse of scents, such as perfume and cologne, that interfere with employees' abilities to concentrate. If such a rule exists in your company, you can send a reminder by e-mail to the entire department without pointing fingers at or singling out anyone in particular.

- *Go to a superior.* If all else fails—whether your suggestions have been ignored, forgotten, or just not taken seriously—you should go to your manager and ask him how the problem should be handled. If it's truly affecting your work, then there is indeed an issue there. "A few of us are having difficulty with Penny's perfume. It's so strong most days that some of us routinely feel nauseous or experience headaches. We've politely asked her to tone it down, but she is not taking our request seriously. I don't want Penny to think we're ganging up on her, but it's difficult to concentrate under these conditions, and I'm hoping you'll be able to address this with her."

Keep in mind that there are scents everywhere—from the subtle to the strong. You can't complain about everything, but one good barometer is the opinion of your peers. If you are all in agreement that a scent is offensive, then you have adequate reason to approach the offender or your manager for relief.

How to Ask a Colleague to Pick Up After Herself

A messy desk holds more bacteria than a toilet seat. This is true even if we just consider paperwork, without taking into account any scraps of food left on the desk. It's no wonder that so many people get sick at work—they're either sick literally from being around a mess, or they're sick figuratively from having to put up with or clean up a mess.

WHOSE MESS IS THIS? There are different ways that your colleagues may disrespect the workplace. He allows his coffee mug to leave stains on every desk he visits. She allows tons of clutter to pile up, which makes the open-office environment look like a pigsty. The break room has dirty dishes in the sink and old lunches in the fridge. A coworker leaves paper towels all over the restroom sink. Extra paper is left alongside the copy machine, and empty cartridge boxes sit by the fax machine. These are signs of being lazy or inconsiderate, or perhaps busy and unaware.

These messes aren't onetime occurrences. Your patience has grown thin, and it's time to speak up. You can get the results you seek without offending anyone if you handle the problem tactfully.

SIDE EFFECTS OF MESS. Mess results in disorganization and a cluttered workplace, and workers and those around them get irritated. Mess creates feelings of anxiety in workers by forcing them to hunt for missing items and clean up after others while necessary work goes undone.

By working in a messy environment and having to look for things you've lost or misplaced, you can actually waste a chunk of your day—a productivity loss that definitely costs the company money.

You can ask a colleague to change by pointing out the behavior and offering solutions:

- "If you kept your files in order, you wouldn't be late for the project meetings. I found one of your files by my desk and another in that office. I know color-coding files works for me. Perhaps you should try that."

- "I know your work is very important, but it's spread out all over the place, which often makes it difficult to access drawers and equipment. Would you be able to organize and stack it daily so that I'll be able to get to the files I need?"

- "You're a great worker, but so much clutter and garbage are unsightly. Would you be able to tidy up your work space each day?"

STILL MESSY. Sometimes your coworkers may need gentle reminders, since bad habits are hard to break and everyone gets busy and has a tendency to lose track of what he or she may be doing or not doing. Model the behavior you'd like your colleague or colleagues to emulate. Make sure your work area is clean and neat. Pick up after yourself in shared work areas such as copy rooms, break rooms, and restrooms.

You might also initiate a weekly or monthly office or department-wide cleanup. Some companies bring in dumpsters or distribute oversize garbage bags each quarter to encourage everyone to regularly get rid of useless materials and eliminate clutter. This prevents any one person from being singled out, as it requires a group effort, with compliance and participation from everyone.

Ask the office manager to routinely purchase and distribute disinfectant desk cloths, keyboard cleaners, antibacterial hand gel, and other supplies, including file folders and desk accessories, that encourage cleanliness and organization as a way of office life.

How to Ask a Colleague to Stop IM-ing You

Instant-messaging (IM-ing), although not universally endorsed or approved by employers as a proper way of communicating with clients and colleagues, remains one of the top ways of staying in immediate contact with them. With the luxury of technology comes the responsibility to avoid the potential for both negligence and inconvenience. Keep in mind that the majority of employers now monitor all electronic activity, which includes all IMs that you send and receive on the company's computer system. This means that the volume of your messages shouldn't be your only concern; their content is even more important.

U.S. businesses are experiencing a decrease in productivity worth billions of dollars per year due to unnecessary interruptions from e-mails, IMs, the Web, and telephone calls. It can cost any worker, from the entry level to the executive, a good chunk of her time every day—much of it due to nonurgent communications.

When people receive IMs, they usually cannot differentiate between urgent and important, or they don't take the time to think about it. You hear the ding or see the flashing box pop up, and you naturally move to check it out.

U THERE? It's as if your every move were being watched, since inevitably you sit down at your desk and almost immediately the box pops up onscreen, asking, "U there?"

The majority of your colleagues know when instant-messaging is too much, and you're not afraid to tell colleagues that you're busy and can't chat. But sometimes there are one or two people who either don't get it or just can't stop. They're addicted to IM-ing you about every little thing.

IM ETIQUETTE. There are some simple technology tools that can shut down a conversation, as well as diplomatic ways to let someone know you're otherwise engaged.

- *Block the messages.* Depending on the messenger service you have, there are plenty of automatic messages that will let IM-ers knows that you're not available. Among them: "Busy," "On the phone," "Away from my computer." Yes, you will eventually hear from your buddies, but at least they cannot interrupt you during the time block you have set aside for uninterrupted work.

- *Don't be anxious.* You don't have to answer an IM just because it pops up. Take a breath, consider who it is, and see exactly where you're at in your work. If the message isn't important, ignore it and close the window.

- *Consider how important any particular message is.* If you use IM to communicate for business, there will be messages that require immediate handling. Take a few seconds to discern which ones should be addressed and when.

DEAL WITH THE CULPRIT. If your IM-er is constantly firing off one-liners telling you the latest gossip, asking you about the lunch menu, inquiring about the boss's whereabouts, or chatting about last night's TV shows, you must deal with the interruptions, or they'll continue. You can ask the coworker to stop. Say, "As much as I could easily IM back and forth all day, if I did, it would be impossible for me to get my work done. I'm cutting back significantly, and I'd appreciate it if we both tried to restrict our messages to important business topics only."

If your colleague does not cease or reverts to IM-ing you about trivial matters, IM her back with short, firm messages. "Can't chat. Remember: important stuff only." Answer fewer and fewer of the messages until she gets the point.

You can also inform her that your company monitors all IMs and that it's probably against e-policy to engage in excessive communication about nonwork topics. Continuing to chat could cost you your job, and you would appreciate her understanding.

If she doesn't get the point and continues IM-ing you, you can block her permanently on your recipients' list to prevent her messages from getting to you. When she calls or e-mails you to ask why you've taken this action, let her know that you asked politely for her to stop sending trivial IMs, and that your request was ignored. You took this action to improve your productivity.

If you sense that incessant IM-ing is an office-wide problem, consider asking management to remind all staffers about the e-policy that limits usage of this form of electronic communication. In the absence of such a policy, consider initiating one. You can then say that too-frequent IM-ing is not only a waste of time, but against company policy as well, and most employees take company policy seriously.

How to Ask for a New Boss

When you have an authority figure running the shop who has a wealth of knowledge and expertise, it's great to be able to seek advice and guidance from that person and to work with her toward a common goal. But what happens when you constantly butt heads with your boss, never seeing eye to eye with her? What if her style is inhibiting your growth and damaging your morale? If you're convinced that the relationship is beyond repair, then it's highly possible that one of you must go.

WHAT THE X?#*@?! With so many varying environments, work styles, people, personalities, and goals, there are any number of reasons why things in the office can and do go wrong. It takes a leader—a great boss—to minimize the conflict inherent in those factors and enable her team to maximize their individual and collective talents for the good of the business. But sometimes the boss doesn't cut it, and her style undermines everything you have to offer.

BIG DEAL OR NOTHING MUCH? Overall, some bosses can be unsympathetic, overbearing, or verbally abusive. They can be buck passers, deadline dodgers, or slackers. Other times, they can just be perfectionists, and for whatever reasons you ended up on their wrong side. Most often, you might just have to suck it up and take it. For example, you may hear, "Where the hell are those reports? Dealing with you is like talkin' to my kid." Depending on the industry, this could be viewed as abusive or dismissed as bluster. Someone could argue that this is a healthy display of frustration on the part of a creative mind. In another line of work, the boss could be reprimanded for being a jerk.

TAKING ACTION. If your environment is intolerable, and you've decided that you need to move on or that your boss needs to be put in her place, get your ammunition ready and proceed with caution.

- *Gather the evidence.* You must document disturbing behavior—from conversations you've had to the way you have been treated. In a journal—not the company computer—list the details of the incidents, including dates, times, specific language, tone and style, and any witnesses. Keep in a private file hard copies of memos and e-mails that support your position.

- *Find occurrences involving coworkers.* Do any of your coworkers have similar complaints? Do they have complaints of a different nature that nevertheless support your position that the boss is inefficient? When they share stories and frustrations with you, note down the incidents.

In an ideal world, you'd be able to sit down with your boss and talk it out. But that isn't always possible. Before writing off the possibility of talking things through, try having a candid and direct conversation in which you explain why you're not happy and what you'd like to see changed.

For example, you might say, "When you berate me in front of my colleagues, as you've done repeatedly, it shows a lack of professionalism on your part and also embarrasses me. If you're unwilling or unable to change, I will have no choice but to ask for a change of assignment." This implies that either you'll be moved to another department, or the boss will be replaced. That's a decision senior management would have to make after evaluating your complaint.

Another option is to ask your manager how he or she perceives you and your performance. Use that conversation as a springboard for discussing how his or her style and demeanor prevent you from operating at your fullest potential.

When a direct approach fails to produce any change for the better, you can bring the matter to human resources. Keep in mind, however, that human resources isn't there to serve and protect your interests. That department exists to promote the needs of the company, which may require your boss to stay right where she is no matter what.

You can ask human resources for assistance by presenting your facts and not allowing emotion to get in the way. "I have a delicate and challenging situation to discuss with you. There are a number of my colleagues who feel exactly as I do, which is why I'm coming to you now. Our manager is increasingly difficult to work for, and it's hurting morale and impacting our ability to perform our jobs effectively. I have several specific examples to share with you, and it is our hope that a change can be made."

One strong basis for pursuing a complaint against your manager removed would be evidence of unethical behavior or illegal activities. In a corporate climate that is acutely aware of the importance of adhering to the highest code of ethics and avoiding any signs of impropriety, top management should have a zero-tolerance policy for such behavior, which includes expense fraud, accepting expensive gifts in exchange for favorable treatment, excessive drinking or drug use in the workplace, intentionally cutting corners, ignoring regulatory issues, engaging in sexual harassment, or otherwise violating company policy. Keep in mind, however, that any decision to report an employee for alleged wrongdoing is a delicate one.

She Asked for It!

I know what it is to not get what you want. At a previous organization, I asked for a raise. My supervisor never once told me that I was worth it or that the finances didn't allow it. She just said, "We don't give raises here." That really made an impact on me, because it made me feel devalued and underappreciated. I didn't *need* a raise, but I did need the affirmation that I was worth a raise and that my contribution was meaningful. When I turned in my resignation, she halfheartedly asked me if there was anything she could do to change my mind, and I said no, but I thought, *The one thing you could have done—and it would have kept me here—was tell me that I deserved a raise and that you would give me some small token, even though money was tight.*

—NORRINE RUSSELL, Ph.D., executive director, the Ophelia Project

How to Ask for Consensus

Walk down the corridor of any corporation these days, and you're likely to hear talk of building consensus. It's a new buzzword built on an age-old notion. When you build consensus, you build support. Rather than going into a meeting and presenting a new idea cold turkey, the goal should be to discuss it with some key players ahead of time. You get their buy-in so that when you present it, you already have endorsers on board. If they are influential within your company, you are more likely to get approval from the larger group. Think of this as being along the lines of securing impressive references to vouch for you and your work ethic when you are job hunting.

Before you panic—wondering how you'll be able to pull this off since we've also encouraged you to hold onto your ideas and maximize your chances of getting that long-overdue credit—keep in mind that you've been building consensus since you were a kid, whether it was soliciting a sibling's support in approaching your parents for a special treat, or getting a few friends together to help you persuade the others to see things your way.

Building consensus becomes increasingly important as you mature in your career and gain seniority. Executives at the top levels of their companies must make their strategies inspiring to employees at every level. Yet it's never too early to begin learning and applying the same tactics and theories to your own career. You want to build consensus for two key reasons:

- You can produce valuable support for your idea.

- You can start a flow of meaningful communication.

Generally, you build consensus for ideas that are new and different. For example, you may be working on an advertising campaign for a watch manufacturer. You were asked to create a campaign around the company's classic, timeless image, which appeals to affluent, middle-aged buyers. However, you have a hunch the watches are now being worn by trendy, wealthy twenty-somethings. You want to create fresher, edgier ads, believing this will appeal to a broader market.

BE ARMED WITH FACTS AND FIGURES. Before you make your proposal, however, you need to build consensus among the people who will be integrally involved in the creative and decision-making processes. Begin by sharing your data with team members and immediate supervisors. For example, "I've discovered that the fastest-growing market is this young buyer. For example, new data show this market has doubled over the past year. This is the fastest-growing market, and it now comprises one out of every three buyers. Our research shows the watches are being worn at upscale nightclubs in New York City, Los Angeles, and London. They are also showing up on the wrists of young Hollywood. How do you feel about taking our ads in this direction?"

You know you're on track when you sense growing support for your idea. Later on in the process, you may be more direct in building consensus. This doesn't mean you should let everyone else get credit for your idea. However, it does mean working in a team; getting your client, coworkers, or superiors to buy in will help you reach your goal. For example, you may approach the client by saying, "We've been talking about taking the campaign in this new direction, and we want to discuss this with you during the meeting next week." Again, be armed with facts and figures to support your idea. Anything that supports the bottom line is going to capture their attention for sure.

TIMING IS EVERYTHING. You want to avoid catching people off guard. In a worst-case scenario, you end up building consensus in the wrong direction. Opinions are formed against your proposal without your argument ever having been fully heard.

Your safest strategy is to build consensus step-by-step. Start with peers and work your way up. If necessary, use graphs, newspaper clippings, statistics, and reports to make your case. Start building consensus early and look for opportunities to present your views casually. Say to a peer, "The client's watch appeared in the newspaper's style section this week. I really believe we need to focus on this younger demographic. What do you think?"

SENSITIVE ISSUES. You may also want to build consensus because of a problem. For example, you may find the lack of company-sponsored child care problematic. In this case, you would build consensus among other working parents inside the company. You might then say to your supervisor, "The lack of company-sponsored child care is straining my family's budget, and the issue frequently weighs on my mind. I've discussed this with several other working mothers and fathers here, and they all have the same concern that I do. We'd like to have a candid conversation with you about our thoughts and findings."

Don't use the support you've built as a majority-rules tactic. Avoid saying, "I've spoken with all 23 of the working mothers in this organization, and we are in agreement that something's got to be done." You don't want to come across as heavy-handed. When you have built consensus, you have a strong position from which to begin a dialogue, but never abuse that advantage.

CHALLENGING SITUATIONS. Building consensus is especially important if you know you're going to advocate a controversial idea. For example, while your research shows that the general buzz is in favor of adding company-sponsored child care to the benefits package, it also shows that paying for child care would not be in the company's best interest because of the considerable cost. You're going to take an opposing position on this proposed plan. Instead of resigning yourself to being the lone naysayer at the big meeting, explain your rationale privately in advance to a few trusted colleagues. Don't catch them off guard when you make your views public. By meeting with them one-on-one in advance, you'll give them the opportunity to grill you, and you'll have a chance to address their concerns in a nonadversarial environment. There's a good chance you'll win them over in time for the main meeting and be able to count on them to lend credibility and support to your position.

She Asked for It!

For me in the early days of my career, the key to asking was to determine who had the best chance of making something happen. I always asked myself, *Who might help us get what we need?* I'd team up with the individual who had been there the longest, and he'd present the idea on our behalf as being partly his idea, too. That clearly gave my request the best chance at being granted and put the odds in my favor.

—DR. DOROTHY MITCHELL-LEEF, *reproductive endocrinologist and infertility specialist*

How to Ask for Less Responsibility

You love your career, you enjoy working for your company, and the position and title you have are extremely rewarding. But lately it seems that either you have bitten off more than you can chew, or your coworkers delegate tasks to you, or the boss relies on you to deliver too much. Instead of burying your head in misery, speak up and get clear on your workload and responsibilities.

REASONS YOU HAVE TOO MUCH TO DO.

- A boss or colleague is trying to pass the buck.

- You are trustworthy and dependable, and others often pile more on your plate.

- You are a control freak and do not know how to delegate. You have gotten yourself into a jam by taking on more responsibility than you should have.

- You're behind in your work by your own fault, although it's not your typical problem.

- You have a personal issue that is impacting your ability to get work done.

REASONS YOU'VE DECIDED YOU MUST LESSEN YOUR LOAD.

- Something is going on in your life: you've gotten married or divorced; you have an ill family member or a new baby.

- You've been placed on warning.

- You know someone is "passing the buck," and you must put your foot down.

- The quality of your work is declining.

WAYS TO ASK FOR LESS.

- Seek a coworker's help. The need might be temporary or permanent, depending on the amount of work you're facing. Ask for assistance by saying, "I'm bogged down with multiple priorities. Since I don't want anything to fall through the cracks, I'm hoping you'll be willing to lend me some help by handling a couple of the tasks."

- Reject the one who is handing off the work to you. Ask for less work at the moment someone asks you to handle a task. Don't wait until you're saddled down before speaking up. "I must stop you right there. Although it would be my pleasure to help you if I could, I'm already at full capacity in terms of how much I can accomplish at this time."

- If you are a control freak, learn how to delegate. Tap into the skills and strengths of the people around you. Surely you know that there are people who can manage some of the same things you can. Establish deadlines and expectations so that both parties will be satisfied with the outcome.

- Rediscover your job description, or remodel your position. When the load seems insurmountable, have a candid conversation with your manager in which you detail all of the work you've been expected to handle. Prioritize what you believe to be the most important and challenging tasks. Ask that the work you can't manage be given to someone else. Explain that if you're required to continue to handle it all, something will suffer, which would negatively impact the entire department.

RESPONSIBLE ADJUSTMENTS. If entirely too much work is something you've gotten yourself into, then it's up to you to develop a mechanism for determining just how much you can handle. While the realization that you can't do it all may put a dent in your ego or disappoint your boss, those negatives will soon dissipate because true responsibility is about proper accountability.

- Prioritize the most important projects that must be completed.

- Revisit your job description and compare it to the current reality of your daily load.

- List those extras that you either spend too much time on or that can possibly go to someone else—either temporarily or permanently.

- Have a meeting with your boss to discuss your responsibilities and why you need to have less work. When asking your boss to help you lessen your load, offer a solution. When you present the problem and the suggested scenarios for fixing it, there's a better chance of having your request approved. Some options: "On Thursdays I know Tina always has some free time. Can I give this project to her? She's very talented in this area and would no doubt do a great job." You can also try saying, "I know I make things look easier than they really are, but I have to overcome my willingness to take on more work than I should. I'm hoping you can help me to delegate effectively."

How to Ask for an Extension on a Deadline

Asking for an extension is difficult in today's highly competitive workplace. People are under a lot of pressure, and they often want everything yesterday. Yet sometimes at work you will find that you are falling behind on a project or that the scope of the work is wider than you anticipated. You worry that the quality of your work may be affected by a tight deadline. So you consider asking for an extension. At this stage, you need to weigh a variety of factors.

- What is the reason for the deadline?

- Do you perceive flexibility with the deadline?

- Will your client ask for a reduced fee if you miss a deadline? Will you be penalized by your boss?

- What will the effect be on the other people involved in the project?

You also need to ask yourself, "What will be scrutinized when this project is finished?" Quite often, the speed at which you completed an assignment is forgotten. Everyone's focus is ultimately on the quality of your work, which means you'll find little sympathy when you try to defend an error by saying you had a tight deadline. In such a case, you often need to endure the discomfort of asking for an extension. You may make some people mad, but if you have used good judgment and deliver strong results, you will find your reputation quickly restored by the quality of your work.

OFFER A SOLID RATIONALE. When you ask for an extension, give solid professional reasons for needing it that show benefit for the company. For example, "The project has been delayed because the client has not yet signed off on our estimate. Once we have their approval, we will need a week to finalize the project." Another option when asking for an extension: "The supplies we received are inferior to the ones we'd like to use. It will take another 48 hours to receive the proper shipment, and then another 2 days to implement the changes." If the problem is related to staffing, you might say, "Our graphic artist on this project has been out sick for a few days. We weighed the option of bringing in a replacement in order to get this job done on time; however, since she's up to speed on the vision and goals, we'd prefer an extension of another week."

ASK FOR PERSONAL REASONS. Sometimes you will have to ask for an extension for personal reasons. You have obligations outside of work that may interfere with your professional responsibilities. In this case, be straightforward and brief. Provide some detail, but not too much. "My child got sick, and I was unexpectedly out of the office for two days. That has caused me to fall behind on this project. However, I will have everything by Monday." Avoid weighing down your request with lots of emotion. Don't expect a sympathetic response or a pat on the shoulder. When you ask for an extension, you are probably throwing off someone else's schedule. Be sensitive to that, and always try to avoid asking at the last minute.

WHEN YOU MISS A DEADLINE. There may be a rare time or two when you simply overlook a deadline. In this case, be up-front without offering an excuse. Before hastily committing yourself to a new deadline, carefully review the scope of the remaining work. Examine what's been done and what remains, and figure out how you'll complete the remainder with the quality that is expected. Ask for enough time to deliver results that will satisfy everyone, even though your request may upset people who would prefer a quicker turn-around. Simultaneously, keep in mind that sooner or later everyone has to move mountains and work around the clock to meet deadlines.

You might say, "I missed the deadline, and I apologize. This is when the work will be done." Or, "I don't have an excuse to offer you, but I take full responsibility for my tardiness in delivering this report. I will work throughout the weekend to get it done, and you'll have it Monday morning."

How to Ask If You Are About to
Lose Your Position

There is a high degree of uncertainty in the workplace today. Excellent performance alone won't guarantee your position with an employer indefinitely. Shifts in the economy have precipitated a free-agent nation. The upside is opportunity for anyone with the wherewithal to seize it. The downside is less professional security overall. You must learn to manage change by sensing it and asking questions.

Asking at the right time whether your job is secure can actually save it. Phrase your question according to the situation. Key reasons why you could lose your job include economic factors, poor perfor-

She Should've Asked for It!

In many instances, I didn't ask for help and more time to get it right.

When I was a senior producer at *Good Morning America*, I was often suggesting elaborate segments to help our show become a huge success. But oftentimes I bit off more than I could chew. In one instance, I wanted us to do a segment about daughters-in-law who hated their mothers-in-law. I booked a pair who had some degree of vitriol, but it was not as much of a family feud as might have been expected.

At the last minute, inspired by Diane Sawyer's request that I make this the best television segment it could be, I canceled the guests, and on very little notice and with no help, I tried with great gusto to find another pair who had the animosity to make the segment really illustrate what we were getting at.

Unfortunately I was too proud to say that I needed more than one day to do it. Although I was able to find other guests for the segment, it was not nearly as successful as it could have been. I let down not only myself, but also the anchor of the program and the millions of viewers who were watching. So asking for more time and for more help is something I have since learned is essential when you are trying to get it right.

—LISA SHARKEY, *president, Al Roker Productions*

mance, a merger or acquisition, new management, or a new boss. Sometimes it's just the luck of the draw.

DURING TRANSITION. Whenever a company goes through a major transition, employees are unsettled. Information voids precipitate gossip. People worry about receiving pink slips. Entire departments could be wiped out—a possibility that is naturally difficult for the employees to contemplate. The best advice for handling times like these is to be proactive. Don't bury your head in the sand.

In an environment like this, it may seem naive to ask whether your job is secure. You may wonder, *Isn't that what everyone is asking himself?* But the key is how you ask. When you do ask, you essentially want to campaign for your job. Make the case for people to keep you around. Demonstrate your willingness to adapt to change. Highlight your unique worth to the company.

You might approach your new boss and say, "I like the changes initiated by this new management team. I know you'll want many of your own people in management roles, but I wanted to share with you the unique strengths that I bring to my position." Talk about your excellent contacts or underscore your relationships with clients, vendors, or service providers. You could also ask, "What are your intentions going forward?"

By doing this, you will be able to take action early if the news is not positive. Quite often, however, you won't receive a definite answer. Such vagueness is characteristic of transitions. Yet even if you leave a meeting without an answer, you have made a case for your new boss to keep you around.

ECONOMIC FACTORS. Use a similar approach when your company is hurting financially. The first step is to acknowledge that change is happening. For example, you might approach someone in senior management and say, "I know that the company has lost some business and that times are rough financially. I wanted to share my support as well as how my skills and abilities are valuable to the company, especially in this challenging period." In this case, you are not asking directly, "Is my job secure?", but you are strengthening the case for your employer to keep you and showing your concern for the business as well as for what your boss might be going through. To further strengthen your position, you might do the following:

- Highlight your institutional knowledge.

- Show how you can bring in more business.

- Stress how you can save the company money.

- Prove that losing you will cause a hassle and a headache.

- Suggest a plan of action to stave off losses and spearhead growth.

- Increase the number of your responsibilities.

If you aren't already involved in boosting the company's bottom line, consider getting involved. It would be hard to justify letting you go while you are increasing revenue.

PERFORMANCE. You could also be terminated because of poor performance. In this case, it is important to present a performance plan, along with a definite time frame, for how you'll dramatically improve your work. You might say, "I recognize that aspects of my performance have not been up to par. I would like to talk to you about initiating a plan and some specific goals that I can set out to achieve in order to improve my performance." Show that you are going to make quick and positive changes and that you can surmount the problem. Many companies are very forgiving when someone has valuable skills.

However, if your performance is suffering, you are unhappy in your current role, and management is equally displeased with you, you might want to ask about their willingness to offer you a package in exchange for your resignation. Without admitting fault or pointing blame, ask by saying to your manager or your human-resources representative, "Would you be agreeable to discussing a package in exchange for my resignation?"

DON'T BE AN OSTRICH. Companies today exist on shifting sands. Burying your head in the sand is not the solution for handling change. When you sense trouble at work, address it by being alert, aware, and proactive. If you must argue for your position, don't shy away from doing so.

How to Ask to Be Included in Meetings

Attending the right meetings at work can increase your visibility with the company's decision makers. You can raise your profile and show your value just by arriving prepared and by contributing. However, you may not be invited to every meeting that you want to attend. In that case, you should ask to attend. When you do this, show why your participation in the meeting would be of value. You might say to your boss, "I know you will be pitching the client next week. I contributed a lot of design work to the pitch and would very much like to see how it is received. I would also like to be available in the event someone has a question. May I tag along?"

MAKE REQUESTS. Never let the lack of an invitation to a meeting stop you from asking to attend. Generally the reason you weren't invited is an insignificant one, such as the planner's thinking she already had enough people attending or assuming you weren't interested in the topic—the agenda may be focused on issues outside of your core competency.

Depending on the subject and participants, you can announce your intention to attend the meeting, or you may ask to join in. When appropriate, especially for gatherings involving senior management, argue that your presence will add value. Say to your boss, "I know you are meeting with the CEO next week to discuss the new product. I'm starting to receive calls from the media about this. I would love to join you, share what I've heard, and discuss the angle at which I should be presenting the information publicly."

BE OF VALUE. Alternatively, you might have knowledge that you could expand upon by attending a particular meeting. In this case, talk about the long-term benefit to the company. Maybe you are assisting the investor-relations department with the annual report, and there is an upcoming meeting that you want to attend and that involves the board. Take a similar approach by stating your contribution to the project and asking to join in. Say, "We've been hard at work on the annual report for the past few months. I know the board is flying in next week. I'd like to attend since I am likely to gain some useful background color that I can capture in the text."

BE VISIBLE. Talent alone is not enough to guarantee success at work. You must find ways to become known to decision makers, but always do so within a strategic context. In this example, a board member may end up impressed by the annual report. Although many people collaborated on it, he will identify it with you because he met you. He may soon be in need of a speechwriter and may contact you because he likes your work. This is how many great careers are built. The process is rarely a steady climb based on talent alone; you need to combine talent with smart networking.

On the day of any meeting, be prepared. Know the agenda and the participants in advance. If you're new to the group, ask for the opportunity to introduce yourself and to share briefly your interest in participating. This is a great chance to showcase your talents and your position within the company.

How to Ask to Be Excused from a Meeting

A common complaint in the corporate world is that there are too many meetings. As you progress in your career, you will likely want to limit the number of meetings you attend. However, keep in mind that while people at meetings might seem to waste time debating issues without determining resolutions, meetings do offer you a valuable chance to share your ideas, build meaningful relationships with colleagues, and showcase your leadership skills. The value of those opportunities should not be dismissed.

If you want the boss to excuse you, there are some practical ways to insure that he does so. The first is to simply offer a legitimate reason why you can't attend. This may be another commitment or a deadline. "I can't attend the weekly planning meeting tomorrow. I have a conference call. One of our vendors backed out, and we have to discuss our next steps." Or, "I can't attend the meeting tomorrow. We have a quick turnaround on the ad campaign this week. We need to present to the client this Friday."

She Asked for It!

Keep in mind that when you ask, it's not the end of the world if you don't get what you want. That you were turned down doesn't mean you can't ask again. You have to be aware of why you were turned down. Perhaps you were so anxious that you didn't pay attention to timing. I can think of all sorts of occasions when someone asked for something at the wrong time—maybe he wanted a new computer or a raise at a time when a division hadn't met its numbers for the quarter—and that person dropped in my esteem because he only saw the small picture.

Smart people put off negotiations until the atmosphere is right. The time to ask is when things are good. You don't ask when everyone is walking around worried. There are a lot of people who only see themselves. It's like children—they know when to ask, and they know when not to ask. You don't ask in the middle of a fight between Mom and Dad. Timing is everything.

—GAIL EVANS, author, *Play like a Man, Win like a Woman*

BE DIRECT. On other occasions, it is reasonable—and sometimes advisable—to simply ask be to excused from a meeting. "I've discovered that I can't add very much to the planning meetings, and you seem to have it covered." Or, "I'd like to suggest that I only attend the planning meetings every other week, when you discuss sales and marketing data. The editorial matters don't really involve me." You may also include your supervisor in the decision making by saying, "I need to follow up with the client on Monday morning. The planning meeting doesn't really involve me. Do you mind if I spend the time on this other matter?"

Prove that your time and attention are needed elsewhere, and you will find that most people are supportive of your request. Sometimes you will simply be invited to a meeting as a courtesy. If you don't think you can contribute much to the meeting, say so. "I really can't sit through the meeting next Friday. I have another commitment."

Know, however, that some meetings are worth attending. In cases where they provide you with opportunities to interact with senior management, always try to attend. Don't shy away from joining committees or accepting board positions because they involve meetings. These meetings tend to be concentrated networking or brainstorming sessions and are worth the effort. They bring people together to formulate, consider, and debate new ideas, strategies, or concepts. Have patience for the process.

SET TIME LIMITS. Another way to manage your time at work is to attend meetings for a limited time. This is tricky, as you want to be credited for the time you spent at the meeting, not for the time that you didn't. Announce your intentions to the person leading the meeting. Say, "I'm looking forward to attending the meeting today. However, I have to leave at one-thirty to meet with a client. Are you okay with this?" Show consideration by *asking* to be excused. Then, try to arrive early and remind the planner of your intentions.

WHEN YOU ARE HIGH-RANKING. This becomes especially important when you are high-ranking in your organization. When you are the senior person in the room, you may dampen the spirit of coworkers by leaving early—or by not attending at all. They may think, *She doesn't care about this project anymore*, or, *We just lost our advocate*. In such a case, be sure to announce your intentions at the start of the meeting, or have the moderator do so on your behalf. For example, "We are pleased to have Martha attending today. She is going to update us on sales figures for the fourth quarter and will be here to discuss them with you for the next 30 minutes, after which she'll have to leave this meeting."

RECORD MINUTES. In other cases, when you want to skip the meeting entirely but also want to show interest, ask the planner to have someone record notes on behalf of the the absentees. Ask by saying, "I'm unable to attend the meeting this week, but am very committed to the project. Would it be possible for someone to share the meeting minutes with me?"

WHEN ALL ELSE FAILS. Meetings are a necessary part of all businesses. If you know you do not have time to sit in meetings regardless of the reason, but want to be a part of an initiative, then when you are asked, state up front, "I'd love to serve on your advisory board; however, I'm not available for all the meetings that will be required. Is there any way you could identify the most important meetings and let me know those specific dates in advance? Or, "I want to serve on the planning committee for strategizing new company directions, but I travel so much. Would it be possible to send a representative on my behalf in the event that I can't attend?"

Sometimes you just have to bite the bullet and do your best to contribute your smarts and input to a meeting even if you don't really want to be there. If others can benefit from your presence, that's a contribution worth your consideration.

Personal
Fulfillment

Time Management, Flexibility, and Personal Issues

How to Ask for a Sabbatical or Leave of Absence

There is often a range of personal commitments and interests that leads us to dream of taking off an extended period of time without quitting our jobs entirely. We may want to travel abroad, attend school, write a book, or participate in a meaningful community-service project. Maybe you need time to rejuvenate yourself through a character-building life experience.

WHEN YOU ARE SIGNING A CONTRACT. When you are an upper-level manager or a tenured employee, the best time to ask about a sabbatical is when you are in the process of being hired. High-ranking employees often sign employment contracts that include a provision that allows them to take time off. You'll want to make this a part of your contract as well. Insist on a clause that allows you to initiate a conversation about this issue at a later date.

WHEN YOU DON'T HAVE A CONTRACT. Even when you don't have a formal contract with your employer, you may consider inserting some wording into your acceptance letter that addresses a potential sabbatical. For example, "I may have an interest in finishing my master's degree down the line. That is something that would be good for the organization and good for me. While I would try to configure something within my normal work routine, a second option is to complete the work in an accelerated six-week program." Ideally, your employer will sign off on the terms of the addendum up front.

In a fast-paced, high-pressure environment, there may never be an ideal time to take a sabbatical. However, life events often require us to make this move. When that moment comes for you, sit down with your boss to review several important issues:

- How will this sabbatical benefit you?

- How long do you expect to be gone?

- How will the sabbatical benefit your employer, if at all?

- What is the typical length of time for such leaves?

- Who will handle your responsibilities in your absence?

- Will the sabbatical require your employer to hire someone new?

- Why should your employer ensure you have the right to return?

For example, your spouse is being assigned overseas for three months, you and your children want to join him, and his company is willing to cover all expenses. This is arguably a once-in-a-lifetime experience. You would learn a new language and soak up another culture. Even though you'll be gone for 90 days, you'll return to your employer with a new perspective that could benefit your position.

Or perhaps you're a columnist for a metropolitan newspaper. You have just written a book in which you recount and reflect on conversations you have had with community activists, and your publisher wants you to set about promoting it. You might approach your boss at the newspaper and say, "I have a book due out at the beginning of the year. The publisher wants me to travel extensively between January and May to promote it. Since I will be on the road so much, I wanted to talk with you about my taking a sabbatical."

In either case, explain how your workload can be handled in your absence. Discuss salary and also how your benefits will be handled during this time. Small employers are less likely to have any type of leave-of-absence policy and are more inclined to take a wait-and-see approach to rehiring you. Large employers are more likely to have policies regarding sabbaticals and leaves and are more likely to establish an agreement with you in writing.

Don't miss out on the chance to see the world, obtain a degree, or help a worthy cause because you didn't know how to ask.

How to Ask for the Day Off to Attend to a Child's Needs

Since work typically takes place during the school day, working mothers should prepare themselves for many conflicts over time. They often miss school events because their schedules don't allow for flexibility and they don't want to delegate work.

GIVE NOTICE WHEN POSSIBLE. If you've been given enough notice about a special event, such as a field trip, conference, or per-

She Asked for It!

Many years ago, while I was employed at a previous job, my mom was diagnosed with cancer and given six months to live. She was scheduled to go through some chemotherapy treatments, and I wanted to be with her every step of the way. I needed to ask for a lot of time off to fly out of town, but I was nervous about asking because I worked for a very strict employer. I set aside time to sit down with them and explain my situation. After many difficult conversations, I was given the time off and was able to spend it with my family. I learned so much about myself and my mom during that time, and she's still alive and doing very well. I learned early on in my career that you don't get things accomplished with your mouth shut. Maybe that's why I am on the radio.

—CINDY SIMMONS, host, Star 94 Atlanta's *The Cindy and Ray Show*

formance, ask your boss for a personal day or specific hours off so that you can attend the function. Try not to spring the news at the last minute, especially since such events are typically planned weeks ahead. Depending on your level and seniority, it's often better to ask politely for the time off, instead of announcing that you'll be taking it off; managers appreciate that courtesy.

BE BOLD. Junior high was the time to ask for permission on minute details. But now that you're a qualified, competent business-woman, you get to make the rules—well, most of the time. In the case of major life events, such as the high-school graduation of your child, you do not have to ask permission in a meek manner. For example, instead of saying, "My son is graduating from high school next month, and I'm hoping it's okay for me to miss a few hours of work in the morning," you should say, "My son is graduating from high school next month, so I'll need to take off a few hours that morning, which I'd like you to note on your calendar."

For last-minute or emergency doctor's appointments, nobody would expect you to provide extensive notice. Notify your boss or colleagues by phone or e-mail as soon as you know that your schedule will require an unexpected accommodation, and be sure to show you appreciate it. If you have to stay home with a sick child, make sure you are reachable via phone, e-mail, or both. Doing so might mean you won't have to take an official sick day—your manager might be willing to acknowledge that you worked from home that day instead.

DEVELOP A BACKUP PLAN. When your request for a day off has been denied or you know that a day off is just not possible given your workload, try backup options to avoid missing your kids in action.

- Ask the teacher about attending a dress rehearsal instead of the official performance. That's the best of both worlds: you see your child perform live, and you honor your professional commitments.

- Ask a family member, friend, or fellow class parent to videotape the performance for you. Reserve a special time at home to watch it with your child.

- Ask your child to re-create his part at home for you. You can offer to play along.

- Ask your child how it went and who said and did what, and provide an outlet for him to share his enthusiasm.

- Ask your child on a play date that will be devoted to a special activity. Whether it's visiting a bookstore and reading a favorite story, playing in the park, or chatting over ice cream, both of you will no doubt value each other's undivided attention and affection.

Similarly, if you work an early-morning shift and routinely miss breakfast, or if your work keeps you away from family dinners each night, you can make up for the time in other ways. Ask the teacher to provide you with options, such as volunteering for a school project, helping in the classroom one day, or joining in on a field trip.

DON'T SHOW YOUR GUILT. If missing out on a school event is inevitable, do not draw too much attention to your absence. Making a big deal out of it leads the children to think there's something bad or wrong with Mom not being there, which isn't true.

Men have missed school functions for decades, and nobody questions their commitment to parenting or their role as caring fathers. The same should be true for women: we're not bad mothers if on occasion we must attend to work obligations rather than family ones. Be proud that your children see a mom with a strong work ethic who can pass it on to them.

While the moment may be rife with guilt, don't be unnecessarily hard on yourself. Keep things in perspective and always look at the big picture. No childhood has been ruined by a mom missing a school play, but many childhoods are made more challenging when a mother jeopardizes her job. Working hard and being dedicated to your work enables you to be a better provider for your family.

How to Ask for a Telecommuting Schedule
When a Formal Program Doesn't Exist

Telecommuting has become increasingly popular as telecommunications technology has continued to advance. Various in-depth studies confirm that most employees who work from home are highly productive, and that part of the reason is that they have fewer distractions than office workers and do not have to commute. In some cases, allowing an employee to work at home is a leap of faith on the part of management, because some positions and some employees really are more suited to the office.

CAUTION SIGNS. Even if the thought of eliminating your commute is highly appealing to you, consider what you might be eliminating that you might prefer to keep. Similarly, think about the new challenges you will face.

- Working from home means that you miss out on daily interaction and camaraderie with coworkers. The absence of those relationships can prevent you from growing personally and advancing your career.

- It can be very lonely without the presence of other professionals. Some women thrive on the energy of a bustling office, and when they lose it, they experience feelings of isolation and are unable to focus.

- The distractions of children in your home might prevent you from accomplishing your professional responsibilities. Many companies that allow their employees to telecommute require a working mother who does so to make child-care arrangements. You can't wear your executive and mom hats simultaneously on their dime.

- You might not be disciplined enough to ignore distractions. Say you are working from home and a friend calls from your favorite store to announce a major sale and the arrival of terrific new stuff. Will you be able to resist the urge to drop everything and head over? Will you be able to work without worrying that the plants in your yard need watering?

PREPARE YOUR CASE. Before asking for such an accommodation and before assuming that you'd be happy working from home, consider several key issues:

- Is there a company policy or precedent for such arrangements? If other people are already successfully telecommuting, talk to them about how it works in terms of schedule and daily responsibilities, and how their performances are measured. Success stories within your own company will serve as strong ammunition for your case.

- Research the policies of your company's competitors and the large employers in your area. The findings may support your case.

- Can your work be performed successfully from home? You must determine that your role doesn't require you to be in the main office. A classroom teacher, a retail-sales clerk, and an assembly-line supervisor are examples of people who must perform their functions from a central location. Working from home isn't an option for them.

- Do you have the space? Your dining room table shouldn't double as your office in order for you to be a successful telecommuter. A designated work area, with all of the proper equipment (phone, computer, internet access), is essential. It will help you to separate professional and personal time and to focus.

When you're ready to initiate the discussion, start by asking your manager to schedule a meeting to address the possibility of your working from home. You might say, "I would like to ask you about how we can work together more efficiently. I've been looking at commuting time against the time I'm spending in the office and at home with my family. I'm confident that a smart boost in efficiency for both of us would result from allowing me to telecommute. Is this something you'd be agreeable to exploring?"

If your supervisor is dismissive of this request, saying, "We really need you in the office," you may politely ask why and launch into your justification for such an arrangement. You can introduce success stories and say why you believe you'll be successful and how you expect your performance to be measured. You might also suggest a trial period to permit both parties to test the arrangement. This could range from one day per week for a three-month period to every day for one month, depending on the nature of your work and your rank within the organization. Say, "I'd like to propose that we try this for just one month. I'm confident of my abilities to not only meet but exceed your expectations. I'm aware that you have some hesitancy, and so I'd be happy to supply you with daily reports and updates on my work so that you can monitor my productivity. You won't be disappointed." If, after four weeks, your boss is comfortable with the arrangement, suggest that you switch to a monthly report for the remainder of the year.

When you make the case for telecommuting, stress increased productivity, since that's what's most relevant to the bottom line. Eliminating your commute isn't the paramount concern. Suggest ways that your productivity can be measured. Set benchmarks. If you are a reporter, you may produce three stories a week at work. At home, without the normal distractions of the newsroom, you could produce four. Sell that prospect big-time to your boss in order to get a positive response to your request.

She Asked for It!

Back in the days when few people were telecommuting, I was on maternity leave and wanted to come back to work. I had a plan that allowed me to minimize child-care costs and work from home part of the day. I presented it and negotiated from a place of strength since I was already on staff and knew the lay of the land. I was able to identify for my boss what I could do well from the office and what I could also do well from my home office. I invested in a home office with the latest technology, and it has served me well over the years. I've been telecommuting for 15 years and work in a major marketing position simply because I asked for it.

—MARLA SHAVIN, marketing professional

How to Ask for Work-Schedule Flexibility

A flexible work schedule often allows you to maintain a full-time position with full pay and benefits without operating within the typical nine-to-five routine. You could divide your time between main office and home office, or you could work from either location full-time. You might seek such an arrangement because you're looking for more balance in juggling work and family obligations, but keep in mind that this is an accommodation, not an entitlement. It is important to present in detail how you envision this schedule being incorporated into your corporate culture. It must be a way that allows both you and the company to realize strong results.

BEFORE THE MEETING.

- Create a plan. Be prepared to prove your case with an organized written report that includes your proposed change of schedule, how you'll accomplish your tasks, and any research that backs up your claim that your productivity will increase if you have a flexible schedule. You could show how a lengthy commute affects stress levels and productivity, and propose that by coming in at 10:00 A.M. instead of 9:00 A.M., and by staying until 6:00 P.M. instead of 5:00 P.M., you would be less stressed. Even though these aren't the hours that everyone else works, you'd be able to take care of all of your responsibilities effectively during that time.

- Ask your coworkers about how your company has reacted to previous work-schedule-flexibility proposals. If you have case studies of other employees who've successfully maintained flexible schedules while not alienating their colleagues and managers, use them to your advantage. Managers tend to feel more comfortable when they can cite precedent as a rationale for having granted approval.

DURING THE MEETING.

- Be passionate, positive, and focused when you present your proposal. Never underestimate your power to influence another person. You are a valuable asset to this company, and you need to look and feel like one. If you are unsure of the validity of your request, you'll come across as weak and insecure, which is a surefire way to have the proposal nixed.

- Refer to documented statistics that show how flexible schedules are working in other companies. Many large organizations have adapted work-schedule flexibility to their corporate cultures and are tracking their programs to create data that show their effectiveness. Argue that offering a work-schedule-flexibility benefit helps the company retain valuable employees—including you—and even to attract a better pool of candidates.

- After you have presented your case, ask for questions, and treat each inquiry seriously and with optimism. Remember to ask when to check back for a decision about your proposal.

AFTER THE MEETING.

- Be patient. Avoid the temptation to bug your boss for a decision. You'll only create a negative impression. On the other hand, don't let the issue sit for months. Schedule a time with your employer at the initial meeting to follow up on the proposal.

- If your boss seems hesitant to try this new concept, propose that the company try it with you on a trial basis. Commit to keeping accurate tracking data that show how your productivity has improved, and be honest about any shortcomings of the program.

Remember that by even approaching your employer with such an idea, you are presenting yourself as an innovator among your coworkers, a leader with courage and tenacity. You are opening the door for a vast number of employees who may desire the same benefit, but who may be afraid to ask. Your courage could help you become the person who transforms your corporate culture and turns your company into an industry leader. Consider yourself a trailblazer!

Contributor: Dr. Kathleen Hall, author of A *Life in Balance: Nourishing the Four Roots of True Happiness*

How to Ask for a Reduced Work Schedule

Women sometimes request reduced work schedules in order to achieve a better balance between work and life, and those who change to reduced schedules are generally satisfied even though

She Asked for It!

One of the most important things I asked for was the opportunity to work a four-day week. With four kids and an intense job requiring lots of travel and pressure, I needed a shorter week in order to get some semblance of control back in my life.

I asked for the four-day week during a time when there was a significant amount of change occurring in my department at Nickelodeon. A new senior person had come on to oversee the consumer-products business, and I was the senior member of the existing team, with a great track record. Approving my request benefited both sides in that it gave me what I needed personally at that time and the company retained a key team leader.

Even though I ended up continuing to work a 50-hour week, being home that fifth day enabled me to juggle a senior-level career and the demands of family and home. I wasn't expected to work the fifth day, but was always available for calls or to come in for important meetings. Of course, I ended up doing work on that day and filling in the gaps with late-night e-mails that spilled into the weekend, but there was a big psychological benefit to knowing that the fifth day was not an official workday and that I wasn't wasting two hours on a commute. I did take a pay cut in order to have this schedule, but it was well worth it.

—MAUREEN TAXTER, former consumer-products executive, Nickelodeon they receive less pay. If you are considering such a change, first check into established company policies. Is there any type of precedent? Are there any preexisting programs? It is often in an employer's interest to consider such request, since there can be a substantial cost associated with losing top talent in lieu of addressing work-life issues. Employees tend to stay with a company longer when they are allowed flexible work arrangements. But before approaching the boss, ask yourself some important questions to determine if you're ready to scale back:

- What are your personal goals at this stage?

- Can you and your family survive on your reduced income?

- What are your professional goals?

- Are you willing to plateau professionally?

- If desired, how will you eventually return to the fast track?

- How will you stay connected at work?

- How will you maintain relationships with your boss and coworkers?

- Can you prioritize your responsibilities and manage your time effectively?

SHOW THE BENEFITS. When you ask for a reduced work schedule, you will want to show how this arrangement benefits you and your employer. This is a viable strategy when you have a special or in-demand skill, or when you have a particularly solid relationship with your employer. In some cases, it is more cost effective for the company to allow you to scale back than to risk losing you. In asking for an accommodation, explain why this is important to you both personally and professionally, and how it will benefit the company. Resist the urge to scream, "I'm about to rip my hair out from all the stress of a new baby, and I'm falling asleep on these conference calls because I don't get any shut-eye at night." Instead, focus on why a new arrangement would benefit your employer. For example, "My responsibilities at home have increased with the birth of our second child. I want to continue working at the firm, but I would like to request a reduced work schedule for the next year so that I can enjoy my family and stay connected to my professional interests. Although this means that I will have to accept fewer projects, I will maintain my sharp focus on my existing and future assignments and carry them out with the same level of professionalism and expertise that I've always demonstrated. Would you be agreeable to discussing the parameters of such an arrangement since it would enable you to retain my services?"

Research the competition. As part of your pitch to your boss, include any details about flexible work arrangements offered by leading employers in your industry, as well as those in your area. Include comments from media coverage or information from the company Web sites that speak to these benefits.

OFFER BENCHMARKS. Offer specific methods for measuring the success of the new arrangement. Express your long-term commitment; otherwise, your employer may think that you are considering quitting. Reflect carefully on how the arrangement will work. You must anticipate potential problems ahead of time and avoid them. For example, your new work schedule may preclude your attending certain meetings. How will you stay on top of that information? How will you demonstrate your accountability? What hours will you be available and on what terms? Once you determine what you think you'll be comfortable with and what you're realistically willing to manage given your personal priorities, you can present your thoughts in detail to your manager. Be open to negotiating a middle ground that is agreeable to both of you. If necessary, propose a three month trial period in which both sides will have the opportunity to evaluate the new arrangement.

MONEY MATTERS. You can't expect to work far fewer hours for the same pay. You may be required to take a cut in both salary and benefits. Some large companies have specific protocols that dictate the financial terms. If you're scaling back 50 percent of your workload, you can expect to receive some reduction of your current compensation. The amounts may be negotiated, depending on your seniority and your value to the company. You'll also want to pay particular attention to health insurance, 401k and other savings and investment plans, and paid vacation. Your employer might provide equipment and services for your home office as part of the overall deal.

How to Ask to Be Kept in the Loop
When You're on Maternity Leave

While every expecting mother's focus is on her baby, many pregnant women become worried about being cut out of important business conversations and decisions while on leave. However, there's no need to feel like an outsider. To avoid any unnecessary anxiety, map out a maternity plan and have a candid conversation with your boss prior to the start of your time off. Be prepared with an outline of all of your accomplishments from the last 6-to-12 months, in addition to a list of the

She Asked for It!

While I was working on *The Barbara Walters Specials,* my first baby was born, and I asked to work part-time—four hours a day. Barbara Walters and executive producer Bill Geddie enabled me to have that flexible, mom-friendly schedule for seven years while both my children were small. I was glad that I asked.

When my daughter went to kindergarten, we started *The View,* and my life changed completely. It has only gotten more hectic with *Good Morning America.* Now I am having difficulty asking for assistance and kinder, gentler hours at work because everyone works so hard here, and I don't want to be perceived as a princess.

—JESSICA GUFF, senior producer, ABC's *Good Morning America*

responsibilities that you handle on a daily, weekly, and monthly basis. Put together a 3-month forward-looking calendar on which you've highlighted any important dates or activities that your boss should be especially aware of. Emphasize that you're looking forward to returning to your key role.

To maximize your ability to enjoy your own maternity leave while still remaining connected to your career, here are some key strategies to employ:

- Ask to be e-mailed about important issues, announcements, and decisions. If your work situation entails status reports, ask that you stay copied on them. If it does not, ask a colleague to give you periodic updates. (Once a week might be enough.

Keep your interest and involvement known by a quick note or two back as warranted.

- Be proactive and check in by phone periodically to touch base. It will feel good to stay connected with your colleagues while keeping updated on the office gossip. The personal connection with your coworkers can positively impact your time away and can make for an easier transition when you return.

- Keep current with your industry. Between baby books, exercise the professional side of your brain by reading key trade journals so that you have an overview of any developments, trends, or breaking news within your field. When you see something of note, send an e-mail, place a call, or mail a note and clipping to the appropriate colleague or client. Include your own thoughts on the pertinent issues.

- Offer to assist in a pinch. Technically you're not supposed to work while you're on leave, and you're certainly not required to. However, you might want to consider making known to your boss that in the event of an urgent need, you're available to review a document or answer questions. The more senior your role, the more relevant this becomes.

- Plan a show-off-the-baby visit. Ask your colleagues to select a convenient time for you to pop in. Such a visit can serve as a gentle reminder to everyone that you will be returning. It can also help your colleagues appreciate your commitment to both motherhood and the workplace.

Contributor: Marisa Thalberg, founder of Executive Moms

She Asked for It!

After the birth of my second daughter, I made the difficult decision to return to work full-time following the 16 weeks of maternity leave as the director of publicity for *Late Show with David Letterman*. I made this decision based on my regret over giving up my job at CBS News two years prior, just before the birth of my first daughter.

When the 16 weeks were up, the head of communications for CBS asked me to consider staying on with the network in some full-time capacity. With two kids under the age of two, I almost just gave him a flat no. Instead, I asked him to consider a job share for me and a woman returning from her maternity leave. He committed himself to a 3-month trial. Our job share lasted 5 years. It was the best thing for both of us, for our families, and for the *Late Show*.

—DONNA DEES, vice president, Communications, *New York Daily News*

How to Ask for Honest Feedback on an Outfit

Dressing well shows an appreciation and respect of the setting you're in. Figuring out how to dress well for work is a good investment of time, especially as you work your way up the ladder.

Attire is a subtle form of communication. What is appropriate varies greatly among companies. In some kinds of offices, such as financial-services companies, you'll be on the money if you go toward conservative trends. Wear that same type of outfit into an advertising firm, and you might be considered unimaginative.

Expect a learning curve as you get to know a new environment. Asking a well-dressed colleague for advice can provide valuable feedback. Approach someone with whom you have a noncompetitive relationship, and avoid asking someone who is trying to win your favor, such as a direct report or a salesperson working on commission.

Avoid phrasing your question in a way that will produce a yes-or-no response. Don't ask, "Do you like this outfit?" or "Is this flattering?" You will appear to be looking for affirmation—not honest feedback. Almost invariably, people will try to reassure you. The way you should ask is, "I value your candid feedback on my appearance. How do you think this outfit looks?" Or, "I'm worried that this is not my best choice. Would you give me your honest feedback?" Watch your facial expressions and body language. If you appear to be afraid of the response, the other person may not be completely honest.

In general, you want a polished, clean, crisp appearance at work. Choose quality over quantity. As a woman, you may dread the notion of having to repeat a garment, or—gasp!—a whole outfit in the same couple of weeks. But quality is what people respond to in a professional environment. Invest in a few good-quality items, and learn to mix and match. Other ideas:

- Avoid looking disheveled because of wrinkled or stained clothing.

- Keep your hair neatly cut and styled.

- Keep an extra pair of pantyhose at work.

- Choose clothes that fit and flatter your body type.

- Show personality through jewelry and accessories.

- Err on the conservative side, even on casual days.

- Keep shoes polished and free of scuffs.

- Invest in a well-made handbag that complements multiple outfits.

SPECIAL DAYS. When you want to wear anything outside the norm, ask about it. For example, ask a coworker, "Do you plan to wear sneakers on moving day?" Be clear about casual Fridays or summer attire. Ask about the company policy so that you don't mistakenly interpret "casual" to mean shorts, T-shirts, and flip-flops, when in reality it means khakis, polo tops, and sandals.

She Asked for It!

I manage an intern program that is comprised of very talented college juniors and seniors. Despite their love for fashion and style, this age group is often uncertain about how to dress appropriately in the workplace. Some candidates think that flip-flops and jeans fall under the "business casual" category. We don't require business suits, but part of working in a public-relations firm or in any company is learning the concept of image and perception, so we do require interns to maintain a professional appearance.

Though most of our interns never had a problem with appropriate dress, we once hired one who liked to wear tight, low-cut shirts. I was uncomfortable taking her to events or client meetings.

(continued)

While she was an intelligent hardworking woman, her seductive clothing was not professional.

I had to think hard about how to best approach her. I knew that she needed help with her résumé, so I offered to review it. We discussed her career goals, and I asked her if she'd like some interview tips.

I told her about an intern candidate we once interviewed. The candidate had a phenomenal résumé and sounded professional on the phone. However, when she showed up for the interview, we were shocked to see that her neckline plunged nearly down to her waist. Obviously, I explained, we hadn't been able to hire that candidate because her appearance was not appropriate for the workplace. The intern nodded, and our conversation turned to other career topics.

I observed a noticeable difference in her appearance for the remainder of her internship.

—JENNY CORSEY, senior account executive in public relations

How to Ask If Someone Is Unhappy with You

As a woman, you probably have great intuitive abilities that serve you extremely well in business. It's that special workplace radar that gives you eyes in the back of your head. You must harness that gift. Get enough experience, and you will see that many of your hunches are valid. Your intuition is there to protect you. It gives you the ability to respond to concerns before big issues arise. For example, you may sense an issue brewing with someone at work, but you have no hard evidence yet. You just picked up on changes in his or her behavior. Don't dismiss the concern, but do resist the urge to overreact. Ask yourself, *What precipitated this change? Is this a legitimate concern? Is this person having a bad day? Or does this involve me?* Most of the time it's nothing personal, but worrying about these things can cause you emotional havoc.

ACT ON A HUNCH. If the concern persists and it feels important to you, act on it. You don't know the whole story, so tread lightly. You are simply trying to get information in a nonconfrontational manner. Avoid making accusations. Connect with a compliment, and then state your concern. For example, "Your opinion matters a great deal to me, and I've noticed that you have been very quiet lately. We haven't spoken like we usually do. Is anything going on?"

Avoid asking, "Did I do something wrong?" This puts the focus on you. You are asking for some type of response to make you feel better, which may put the other person on the defensive. Generally, you won't get an honest answer since it's very hard for most individuals to be direct, especially if they are worried about hurting you with the truth. However, the silent treatment can hurt more. The only way you are going to be able to address this concern and make progress is by asking in the right way.

BE DIRECT. If you ask, "Have I done something to upset you?", most people will brush you off, especially if they are angry. That doesn't get you anywhere. Instead, learn to sense delicate situations and to phrase your questions appropriately. For example, say, "Our professional relationship is very important to me, and I would appreciate it if you would be candid in telling me if there is anything that

I can improve upon." Show your willingness to listen by asking for constructive feedback.

MEETING RESISTANCE. Even when you have asked in the right way, you may encounter some resistance. The other person may say, "No, everything is fine." But you may sense some lingering coolness. In this case, you can reiterate, "If there is anything I can do, please let me know. You should realize by now that you can always be straight with me, and that having an honest relationship with you means a great deal to me." Don't grovel or beg for someone to tell you if anything is wrong. You've asked once or twice, which is enough, even if you don't get a clear response.

Other times, someone may respond by saying, "Yes, there is something you have done." In that case you want to have an open dialogue. Be receptive to hearing the criticism, and don't act alarmed or defensive. Respond calmly, since screaming or revealing a hot-and-bothered temper will only inflame the situation.

DEALING WITH YOUR BOSS. Should you sense a problem with your boss, avoid catching him or her off guard. Say, "I would like to set up a time where we can establish that everything is on track." At the time of the meeting, your manager has the opportunity to address whether or not things are going smoothly. If you don't get any sense of his attitude, get to the issue by asking, "Is my work satisfactory, or is there something I should be doing differently?" Don't hide from a potential problem. By being forthcoming about your desire to keep things on track, you will be in a better position to deal with criticism or with change when it comes.

She Asked for It!

Early on in my career, when I was working for a major newspaper, I had a female manager who for whatever reason took every opportunity not to encourage my strengths and who in fact constantly picked on me. I immediately made up my mind that I was going to prove her wrong and decided to give her 200 percent. If she asked me to do something, I'd do it ten times better.

Finally one day, I couldn't take it anymore and asked her the one question that turned everything around. I said, "I'm really trying to do a good job, but it's impossible to do a great job when someone is always putting you down. If there's something you think I should be doing, then could you please just tell me?"

Once I spoke up, she responded with a newfound respect and stopped pushing me around. She knew I was doing a good job, and it was not long after that time that I got a promotion.

—GENIE FREEDMAN, real estate agent

How to Ask for a Good Table at a Restaurant

Everyone has had the experience of having to settle for a bad table — you know, the one by the swinging kitchen door or perhaps adjacent to the restroom. While most restaurants think every table is a good one, that's not always true, and when you're out on an important business lunch, a bad table can be a total annoyance. Perhaps you miss important words because of the clanging of plates, or you're inconvenienced by the hustle and bustle from the kitchen. There are tables that are preferable just as there are waiters and waitresses who are preferable. When a good table is your goal because you're looking to impress an important client or colleague, there is a skillful way to ask for one that ensures your request will be granted.

WHAT'S A GOOD TABLE? It depends on what type of meal you want to have. If you want to see or be seen, you want to have a table in the front or center. However, if you want to have a private, more intimate meal, then perhaps you want a table in a corner.

BE SPECIFIC ABOUT THE TABLE YOU'D LIKE. When making a reservation, be clear about what you want. Avoid saying, "Can we have a great table?" since that's not meaningful to the staff. A better option is to say, "I'm entertaining an important client, and I'd like to have a quiet table away from the crowd. Is this possible?" You might focus on the best service. "I'm having a dinner meeting with very important clients this evening. I'd like to request a table where we're going to receive the best service from your top server. Would you be able to accommodate this?" Expressing what you value as it relates to the table is essential. And don't be shy about letting the manager know that this is your first visit and that you hope to come back.

CONNECT WITH THE RESERVATIONIST. Make your request at the time of the reservation. Call the morning of your date to reconfirm. "Hello, my name is Jane Smith, and with whom am I speaking?" Remind the reservationist of your special request, and then ask, "Will you be there this evening since I'd like to thank you in person?" If not, ask for the maître d's name and ask to have your request relayed to him.

How to Ask for an Upgraded Hotel Room

Today, women are responsible for $1 billion a year of travel spending and comprise half of all frequent flyers. Your home away from home can be more like a castle and less like a hut if you're willing to ask for the best. Hotels are responding with women-only executive floors, antimist backlit mirrors, minibars stocked with facial creams, on-site yoga instructors, babysitting services, and personal shoppers. Living well on the road while working is about learning how to ask for things in the right way. The key word when negotiating with a hotel is *request*. For example, you may be guaranteed a nonsmoking room with two double beds. But you also might want to *request* a room with a view of the ocean, which isn't a guarantee at the discounted rate you're willing to pay.

NEGOTIATE. The first step is to book your reservation at the very best rate. "Are there any special deals during the time of my stay?" You might be eligible for free breakfast, access to fitness facilities, unlimited local and long-distance calls, extended check-in and checkout times, or an upgraded room at no additional charge.

Once you've heard what they have to offer, ask for what you're interested in. "Would you please note in my reservation that I am requesting a room away from the elevator and with an ocean view?" You might also refer to preferences of yours that have been honored when you stayed previously at the same hotel chain. "When I stay at your sister property in Los Angeles, they are always so generous in upgrading my room, which is a great treat when I'm exhausted from business travel. I appreciate that they value my patronage, and I'm hoping you'll consider the same request."

If you're promised any of these special features, be sure to request that the promise be included in the confirmation that is sent to you by e-mail or fax.

CONTACT THE MANAGER DIRECTLY. Send an e-mail or fax letting the manager know that you're looking forward to your visit. Include your confirmation number and reiterate your request. If you are a loyal customer, let him know. For example, "I have a client in Miami, and I visit him monthly. I always stay at your hotel, and I love the rooms overlooking the ocean. Your hotel was fully booked during my last visit, and my request for a room with a view was not honored. I would like to request a room with an ocean view for my visit next month. I hope you'll consider this request." Ask for a reply at the end of your message, and follow up within a week if you don't receive one.

CHECK-IN. If you didn't make special requests prior to your arrival, it might not be too late. At the front desk, treat the clerk politely since he or she is going to select your room. You can ask, "Would you be able to confirm for me that I'm paying the best possible rate for this visit?" You might also say, "I'll be traveling here for business frequently in the next six months, and I'd love to make this my home away from home. Would you be able to offer me a complimentary upgrade so that I can experience the best you have to offer?"

How to Ask About Office Gift-Giving Etiquette

Every holiday, many employees face a dilemma about gift-giving protocol and how to appropriately give or exchange gifts in the workplace, whether with the boss, coworkers, or clients. We all want to be the happy holiday elf of the office, not the non-PC party pooper.

INQUIRE ABOUT OFFICE PROTOCOL. Know your company's gift-giving procedure before the season approaches. Begin by asking the advice of employees who have worked at the company longer than you. Large companies announce their policies in memos or post their gift policies, while other businesses are more relaxed about it, which presents issues. A seasoned office manager or human-resources contact is usually a big help in these matters. If the employees do exchange gifts, ask how much they usually spend. Is there a specific party or time at which gifts are given? Is there anyone who is off-limits for gift giving? Would it be acceptable for you to arrange a group gift for the boss? Determine what it is customary in your workplace, and follow these guidelines:

FOCUS ON YOUR TEAM AND BEING A TEAM PLAYER. If your office allows gifts and there are no hard-and-fast rules, that hardly means you must give everyone you work with a gift. Select the people you wish to gift carefully and avoid giving the gifts publicly, which could make others feel left out. Consider giving gifts to those individuals who help you do your job. Discretely ask fellow employees, "What are some of the best gifts you've been given?" The goal is to get them talking and to learn about their likes and dislikes. Consider initiating a department-wide gift exchange that will take the pressure off personal gift giving. Plan a five-dollar-present swap where everyone brings in a gift or gift card valued at the declared amount and puts it in a big box, and then there is a drawing.

HELPFUL GIFT-GIVING TIPS

- *What do I get the boss?* Avoid one-upmanship or outshining other employees with pricey gifts. If the boss isn't off-limits, consider teaming up for a group gift for him or her. Suggest that everyone contribute an affordable amount to the boss's favorite charity, the name of which you might get from his or her assistant. Donate the collected amount in the boss's honor.

- *What should I get my coworker?* First, ask yourself, *What has this individual done that has helped me at work and made my job more pleasant?* In a thank-you note or card, say how much you appreciate this person and her thoughtfulness. If you still want to get a material gift, consider making it something less formal, like home-baked cookies, a frame to add to her desk collection, or something that reflects her interests. You could also get a gift for her kids or pet instead. Consider what a coworker values and reflect it.

- *What should I do for clients?* Ask your supervisor, "How should I handle our clients during the holiday season? What should I do if someone gives me a gift? How do you prefer I handle this? Are we expected to use our own money to purchase gifts, or does the company make a holiday card available for employees to send out?" You can never go wrong by sending cards with warm holiday wishes. Avoid secular greetings if you are reaching out to a wide audience. You can focus on wishing the recipient success in the new year.

- When in doubt whether or not to give a gift, give praise instead. People rarely ask for it, but when it's well deserved—

when someone at work has assisted you, saved the day, or improved your team—he or she should be complimented. The right words can be free and fabulous.

- And what about office gift-giving etiquette when someone gives you a gift? Rather than be caught empty-handed or totally off guard, have a few modest gifts on hand like gift cards to local coffee shops or bookstores. You never know when you'll want to reciprocate.

A Final Word

While we've addressed a wide variety of questions and answers in this book, we know that along your career journey you're bound to discover new challenges that are unique to you and your position. We encourage you to do your homework before asking for what you want at work. Times and circumstances change, so it's smart to be aware of all the details that might influence your success in getting what you want. If you're unsure of something, get a second opinion from someone you trust who's in a position to lend you his or her expertise.

Since you will no doubt expect others to respond favorably to your requests, look for opportunities to pay it forward. There's grace in asking for help, and there's great personal satisfaction and professional reward in giving it, too.

Please feel free to share your stories of success by e-mailing us at book@womenforhire.com.

We hope that this book helps you to accomplish specific career goals. Be positive, prepared, and persistent, and become one of the women who asks for and gets what she wants at work.